This book is beautifully written, and the honesty in its pages invites the reader's honesty—which is, in my view, one of the best things a book can do. This is a book that will transform you.

SHAUNA NIEQUIST
Bestselling author of *Present Over Perfect*

Steve Wiens is a writer unique in my experience of reading books, and I have read a lot of them. What is unique about *Whole* is that he inserts you (me!) into the biblical story in a way that makes the story convincingly contemporary with us. His children (he has boys), his wife (one wife), and his friends (he has many) become authentically biblical, and we find ourselves living in our own backyards what we previously had only read about.

EUGENE H. PETERSON
Professor emeritus of spiritual theology at Regent College, Vancouver

If you are looking for a simplistic solution to the brokenness you see in the world (and in yourself), this book won't be helpful. But if you're willing to leave the known for the unknown and if you dare to ask the soul-enriching questions found in Steve Wiens's imaginative work, you just might find yourself on the road to wholeness.

RICHARD ROHR
Founder of the Center for Action and Contemplation

I've been lucky enough to sit around a fire in Steve's backyard and talk into the night, and I left that evening feeling as though I'd been breathing fresh air into my lungs. You will feel the same when you read *Whole*. Steve has a gift for telling stories that connect at the deepest level to your own story. This is inspired and compassionate writing that invites us to step into our own promised land.

STU GARRARD
Songwriter and author of *Words from the Hill*

Many authors who brave the subject of brokenness lead us down one of two paths: One glosses over the pain with sugary anecdotes or bulleted prescriptions. The other leaves us wallowing in the pain a bit too long, with perhaps no hope for redemption. Rarely does an author show us another way. Steve Wiens does just that—carving out a new trail where brokenness meets beauty, where humility is a catalyst for becoming whole.

MATT BAYS
Author of *Finding God in the Ruins*

Steve Wiens's book *Whole* stopped me in my tracks. It is a timely, prophetic message not only for the culture and church at large but also for every individual seeking a life of shalom on a deeply personal level. This book forced me to look at others with compassion and gentleness, grace and potential. But more important, it forced me to look inwardly at myself with that same gentle spirit. I'm so grateful for this book, and I look forward to handing out copies to everyone I know along the path to wholeness.

NISH WEISETH
Author of *Speak: How Your Story Can Change the World*

Steve reminds us that it is in the ordinary of everyday life that we are daily invited to experience and participate in the extraordinary. Not extraordinary in the sense of superheroes, but in the simple journey of living into who we were created to be all along. We are the restored ones, and in the sacred mundane of everyday life, we are invited to participate with God in restoring our broken world. This book is not only a reminder of who we are but also an invitation into our collective healing. Let's get after it together.

JON HUCKINS
Cofounding director of The Global Immersion Project

I am a huge fan of pastor Steve Wiens and his savory new book, *Whole*. I tore into it, huge chunks at a time, hoping that his words would heal the hunger in me. Instead, he convinced me that hunger is the lifeblood of being human and that questions are, like bread crumbs, the path to wholeness. If you, too, need fresh perspective on your story, Wiens is a salty sage worth reading.

ERIN LANE
Author of *Lessons in Belonging from a Church-Going Commitment Phobe*

WHOLE

Restoring What Is Broken in Me, You, and the Entire World

STEVE WIENS

NAVPRESS

A NavPress resource published in alliance
with Tyndale House Publishers, Inc.

NavPress is the publishing ministry of The Navigators, an international Christian organization and leader in personal spiritual development. NavPress is committed to helping people grow spiritually and enjoy lives of meaning and hope through personal and group resources that are biblically rooted, culturally relevant, and highly practical.

For more information, visit www.NavPress.com.

For Mary

CONTENTS

FOREWORD

THIS IS A BOOK about wholeness, and as that is the case, I suppose it should start with a caveat: *Wholeness*—most of us don't come by it honest.

In my midthirties, I found myself in a premature midlife crisis. It was not the sort of crisis brought on by the boredom of a career, nor was it born of that time-honored existential question of white middle-class maledom: *Does my life matter?* This was a real crisis, a familial one. The snake eyes of sickness were staring down my youngest son, and who could say whether he'd make it?

Life did what it does—it brought pain to bear—and as that pain pressed and pressed and pressed, everything began to fracture. There were things that—follower of Christ as I was, student of the Scriptures and all—I could have done in the breaking season. I could have turned to the tradition of my faith, could have searched for solace in God's history of restoration, reclamation, and reconstitution. I could have found myself in the narrative of wholeness handed down through the ages. This was not what I chose. Instead, I numbed the pain of cracking up by crawling to the bottom of too many plastic bottles of Gordon's Gin.

This is the straight skinny of my own experience. How many of you have lived a similar experience? How many of you are living it now?

I'm in the dry days now—the days of real *inner sobriety*—and here's what I've found: I've found that even in the fracturing, there is the promise of being put back together. In the days of coming to understand this truth, I began to read Scripture as a participant. I found myself in the story of Job, my own years of loss being restored. I found myself in the story of Peter, whose moment of broken betrayal was redeemed by the risen Christ. I sank into the story of the Christian-murdering Saul—perhaps Christ's greatest reclamation project—and came into wholeness with him on the road to Damascus. I found myself in these stories, and time after time, they worked their magic in me. In the stories, I found the Christ of Scripture, always working for my restoration, redemption, and reclamation. Doesn't he put my broken pieces back together?

This is the beautiful message of Steve's book. We are participants in God's continuing story of whole-making. We've been written into this story no less than Job, Peter, Paul, or any of the characters described in these pages. We are the Living Parables of Christ, the modern personification of God's ultimate promise: *Behold, I make all things new*. Perhaps it could be said this way: *Behold, I make all things whole*.

I wish I'd have known Steve in the darkest days of my brokenness. I wish I could have sat at his table, broken bread with him, and received his invitation to explore the God of wholeness. I wish I wouldn't have had to back my way into the beauty of this understanding. That's precisely why I'm grateful he penned this book. This is his service to the broken—to us—and there's healing in these pages. You'll find Steve writes from a deep well of pastoral mercy, exchanging every "Shame on you" for "Yeah, me too." In that mercy, he calls us from the shame of our fractures and into the story of a kind-eyed, ever-loving, whole-making God.

Read these pages with care. Enter into them with intention. Find yourself descending into the Scripture, becoming a member of the Living Parables. Discover your fractured pieces fusing; feel the fissures healing. Read, read, read, and hear the voice of the God speaking these words over you: *Behold, I make all things whole, even you.*

Even you.

Seth Haines
Author, *Coming Clean: A Story of Faith*

PREFACE

If you're the parent of a toddler, you learn to scan every environment for weapons of mass destruction—basically anything not stuffed. Because if you don't, there's a 100 percent chance your child *will* find that priceless dagger from Morocco and impale the nearest animal, himself, or your foot.

One day when Mary and I were sitting at our kitchen table and *not* scanning for toddlers in danger, our fifteen-month-old son, Isaac, lurched over to us. I noticed something under his tongue, so I put my index finger into his mouth (which is a very offensive thing to do to any other human being but completely normal with a toddler). Because . . . CHOKING HAZARD!

That was when I realized that he had a jagged piece of glass about the size of a quarter in his mouth.

I'd noticed that piece of glass, wedged in the crack between the refrigerator and the wall, a few days earlier. I should have picked it up then, but I didn't. It was there because one of us (I can't remember who) had dropped a large glass bowl, which had splintered into a thousand pieces. That week, we'd swept and vacuumed the floor several times and worn shoes in the kitchen to avoid getting glass in our feet. Yet we had somehow missed that one piece of glass, and it found its way into Isaac's mouth. I pulled it out, and he was fine, but my heart was hammering just thinking about what we'd narrowly escaped.

If only it were always that easy.

When something shatters, the broken pieces find their way into hidden cracks and crevices. Then they end up inside of us, causing pain, especially to the most vulnerable. It's easy to walk past the fragments of brokenness. We're busy and overwhelmed. And maybe that particular piece of jagged glass hasn't hurt *you*. But it is hurting *someone*.

Last night, I watched a video showing a five-year-old boy in Aleppo, Syria, being pulled from a burning building and placed in an ambulance. His home had just been bombed, and he was covered in dust, stunned. The left side of his face was bloody, but he didn't say a word. He didn't cry. He simply touched his face with his hand and then wiped that blood on the orange seat where he sat.

Who is going to pull the jagged glass out of his mouth?

I'm a pastor, and I live in the suburbs, far away from buildings that get bombed. But I see jagged glass everywhere. Last Sunday at church, a dad came up to me with tears in his eyes. "He's back in treatment," he choked out, speaking of his youngest son and the addiction that keeps getting the best of him. I hugged this brokenhearted dad, prayed with him, and held him as he cried.

The Germans have a word that describes the unsettled ache I feel for the brokenness to be made whole—like river water in a jar that keeps getting shaken. *Sehnsucht* is the inconsolable longing for something that you're ardently missing but can't quite name. *Sehnsucht* is what you feel when you get a glimpse of that faraway country and you realize just how far away it is. *Sehnsucht* is a wave that pounds you to the ocean floor and then sweeps you out to sea.

What do you ache for? What keeps you up at night? What can you barely contain?

"Let me tell you a secret," my friend Stefan began his sermon one Sunday. We all leaned forward in our seats. Sermons don't usually start that way. You could feel the *Sehnsucht* in the air.

"I want to change the world."

Stefan preached that sermon eight years ago. Since then, he has started a nonprofit that mentors kids in some of the poorest areas of Minneapolis. His heart breaks when he sees kids in poverty, because he knows that poverty leads to hopelessness and that hopelessness leads to violence. But a mentoring relationship leads to hope. And hope leads to wholeness. Recently, when he was picking up one of his mentees, another boy rode up on his bike and yelled, "Ahh, man! Why can't I have a mentor?"

As Stefan drove away, he watched that boy's image get smaller and smaller. But *Sehnsucht* will bring Stefan back.

What's the secret you long to whisper?

There's an ancient idea that needs unearthing, but it's buried under wars and breakfast dishes and the argument I had with Mary yesterday. It's hidden beneath dusty beliefs and traditions that are now fraying at the edges. The idea is a word, but it's so much more than a word.

The idea is *shalom*.

Shalom is a diamond, and if you hold it up and turn it, you'll see its many facets glinting in the morning sun, sending bright light everywhere. It comes from a Hebrew word that is usually translated as "peace." *Jerusalem* literally means "city of peace."

But let's keep turning the diamond. Let's keep watching where the light goes.

In addition to "peace," *shalom* also means "wholeness, completeness, a state of being unbroken." It's a wedding ring, a perfect circle, even if it's scarred and scuffed. It's the long passage of the sun across the sky as our earth spins on its axis, giving us lush sunrises and expansive sunsets. It's the reconciliation that is forged after a long conflict, when there is genuine repentance and authentic forgiveness.

Shalom is the sense of well-being that comes when brokenness is made whole again.

"In Hebrew, peace-making means whole-making, and not warm-fuzzy-deny-your-concerns-and-stop-being-difficult-making."[1] Shalom is a state of being that is forged in the cooperative work between God and us. Like a diamond, shalom can sometimes look like jagged glass. The journey of whole-making can be dangerous. It's costly. The opposite of *shalom* is the Hebrew word *ra*, which means "evil." It's connected to the word *ratsats*, which means "to crush and break into pieces." Evil, at its essence, is anything that conspires to crush and break into pieces that which was created to be whole. *Ra* creates distance between anything that should be connected together.

Ra fueled the planes that flew into the Twin Towers on 9/11. *Ra* prompted Dylann Roof to walk into the Emanuel African Methodist Episcopal Church in Charleston, South Carolina, where he sat calmly with its members for more than an hour before murdering nine of them. *Ra* marched into Pulse nightclub with Omar Mateen in Orlando, Florida, as he shot and killed forty-nine people and wounded fifty-three others in the summer of 2016.

Ra influenced a man named Cain to murder his brother, Abel. *Ra* persuaded Joseph's brothers to sell him into slavery. It plagued brothers all throughout the book of Genesis.

Ra causes war, deception, and slavery. Whatever else *ra* does, it shatters what was made to be whole.

We've all swallowed the jagged glass of *ra*. But there's something else inside of us, deeper than that, and if it can see the light of day, it will change the world.

You have a secret you want to tell, a whisper of shalom. A whisper of restoration.

I'm a pastor, but even so, it may seem like a stretch to tell you that I think the Scriptures can help you tell your secrets.

The Scriptures hold both pain *and* promise; they're the seeds from which restoration grows. They are shared when great questions are asked, the kind of questions that are strong enough to hold the weight of our secrets.

As you read this book, you'll notice that I'm at least as interested in the questions that are raised in the Bible as I am in the answers that we find. For this reason, I spend lots of time wondering how *this* story relates to *that* one. I believe that the Scriptures tell an overarching story that leads to wholeness, but the Scriptures also include stories of heartbreaking brokenness. We prolong our pain when we try to fix the brokenness without going on a journey of restoration, which includes additional heartache, questions, and long periods of waiting. I point this out because you'll notice that I use my imagination when I write about the stories of familiar characters such as Joseph, Moses, and even Jesus, exploring what might have happened in the white spaces around those black words on the page. I hope you'll see my reverence for the Scriptures humming within those stories.

The Bible itself is whispering something, if we have the patience to hear it. And we are—all of us—caught up in it, whether we know it or not. The stories are sometimes epic and transformative, other times punitive and tribal. And yet the river of the Scriptures flows toward restoring everything that is broken.

Uncovering the secrets buried in the Scriptures will help you tell your own secrets.

Even more than answers, I believe that the Bible contains

some of the best questions in all of literature. I've been a pastor for more than twenty years, and I've savored these questions, allowing them to marinate and become something I hope you will relish.

I love what Krista Tippett has to say about questions:

> If I've learned nothing else, I've learned this: a
> question is a powerful thing, a mighty use of words.
> Questions elicit answers in their likeness. Answers
> mirror the questions they rise, or fall, to meet. So
> while a simple question can be precisely what's needed
> to drive to the heart of the matter, it's hard to meet
> a *simplistic* question with anything but a simplistic
> answer. It's hard to transcend a combative question.
> But it's hard to resist a generous question. We all have
> it in us to formulate questions that invite honesty,
> dignity, and revelation. There is something redemptive
> and life-giving about asking a better question.[2]

In the first part of this book, I ask five of the richest questions found in the Bible. The first three are literally in the text, while the last two are inferred. I took this liberty to make the structure of this first portion less clunky. And, as the great rabbis always said, less clunky is *good*.

Where are you? God asks the man and woman who risked it all and lost it all, and who hid from the one who found them anyway. But this question isn't directed only to them. It's asked of you, too. And it will keep haunting you until you come out of hiding, until you come face-to-face with the one from whom you never need to hide.

Am I my brother's keeper? the murderer asks after burying his brother in a field. It's an evasion, the kind that keeps you behind walls, exposing your fear of the "other." This question pursues you until you recognize that you cannot be made whole until the "other" is also made whole.

What are you seeking? the stranger asks the brother who will be betrayed and left for dead by his older brothers. His answer is the hinge point for the restoration of the children of Israel, and if you follow his lead, it will be for you as well. And for the entire world.

Where are you going? God asks the childless couple before sending them on a journey to an unknown destination with nothing but a promise. This question will lead you away from what is known and into the wild, where sacrifices are made and promises are kept.

What will you bring? Jesus asks his followers before instructing them to bring nothing but trust in the one who sent them. When you set out on the journey of restoration, you'll be tempted to bring a whole lot more than you need. This question invites you to leave behind what is unnecessary so that you can receive something much more powerful.

In the remainder of the book, we will follow the people of Israel as they travel from Egypt, through the wilderness, and finally to the Promised Land. I believe that the journey out of slavery is not only my journey and your journey but also *our* journey.

Shalom is never about just you or me; it's always about *us*.

I tell stories of what happens when people are stuck in slavery or lost in the wilderness or trying to inhabit the Promised Land. I also tell stories about friends of mine—in real life and those I have made in the ancient pages of the Bible. I tell their stories because they have surprised and blessed me with their courage, humanity, and desire for restoration.

I'm intentionally telling mostly stories of *ordinary* people missing and seeking wholeness, because I think most of us believe that we're too ordinary to be swept up in the adventure of wholeness that we see in the Scriptures. So many of us don't believe that our common bumps and bruises of daily life need restoring too. When I coach people on preaching, I encourage them not to use the earth-shattering example (the drug addict who was rescued from the brink of destruction)—not because it's not true, but because most people will be in awe of the story instead of entering it and believing it's for them. I'm taking my own advice in this book: telling ordinary stories in the hope that you'll believe that the story of wholeness really is for *you*.

At the end of each chapter, I've included a benediction—a short appeal for divine help, blessing, and guidance, which is usually given at the close of a worship service. My hope is that it will rise off the page and meet you someplace deep in your heart, giving you something mere words never could. Also included are questions for reflection and discussion. Because, as we often say at our church, "The voice of the chorus is so much better than the solo." Whether you process these questions alone or with friends, I hope they help you go further than my words could ever take you.

A glossary of the main Hebrew and Greek words that I've used is provided because glossaries are nerdy but helpful, and so am I. I had fun with it—adding color, vibrancy, and stories to highlight the meaning of each word—so don't be surprised (spoiler alert!) when you see Taylor Swift's name back there. When you can't quite remember what a certain word means or you want more explanation than I gave you in that particular paragraph, head back to the glossary. You're welcome.

———•———

Maybe you wake up with a fire in your belly.

Maybe you're a quiet caregiver who offers daily kindness to those who likely won't change, whose bodies or minds are sick.

Maybe you're an artist or an author. Maybe you write poetry or make music. Your eyes sparkle when you make something beautiful.

Maybe you're a stay-at-home mama and all you feel is exhausted.

Maybe you're a pastor in the second half of life and you're not sure you can hold on to your fragile faith anymore.

Maybe you're angry.

Maybe you're so full of energy that you're dangerous.

Maybe you're afraid.

No matter who you are or where you live, no matter if you're a raging extrovert or a cautious introvert, the secret that's inside you is there to restore what's broken in me, you, and the entire world.

We need to hear your secret.

Steve Wiens
Maple Grove, Minnesota
SUMMER 2016

WHERE ARE YOU?

Still I'm pinned under the weight
of what I believed would keep me safe.
So show me where my armor ends;
show me where my skin begins.

"PLUTO"
BY SLEEPING AT LAST

I'M SITTING UNDERNEATH the rustic beams of a sturdy deck at a bed-and-breakfast in Somers, Montana, overlooking Flathead Lake. A pair of deer just ambled by, nosing each other in the early morning fog, oblivious of the brokenness in our world, oblivious of the brokenness in me.

I'm looking for something here in Montana. Perhaps what I'm really looking for is *in here*, deep inside me, but it feels elusive, like the deer I just saw. Perhaps it's my secret, wanting to be heard.

I'm in Somers because I won the lottery and got to spend some time with former pastor Eugene Peterson, author of *The Message: The Bible in Contemporary Language* and many other books. His books remind me that you can be a pastor *and* a human being, though it isn't easy.

Eugene said a lot of things during our past two days together, and I wrote down as many of them as I could. He's in his eighties, and his gentle, unassuming wisdom is the kind you lap up like water. I asked him what unique temptations pastors face today. He didn't hesitate with his answer.

"Impatience. Pastors want so badly to be successful *right now.*"

I'm sure he saw me wince, but I tried to hide it.

Later he said, "It's impossible to be a successful pastor. You're a bundle of failings."

When he said those words, I dropped my shoulders, as if someone had just let a little bit of air out of the balloon of my soul, just enough so that I could take a small breath of real air again. But those words also stung, because the truth really does hurt.

Please feel free to laugh out loud at this next admission.

In 1980 our very Baptist family somehow came into the possession of a record by the soft rock duo Air Supply, even though I'm pretty sure we weren't allowed to have secular albums in our house. I played that record over and over again, singing loudly along with the melancholy melodies, all of which were designed for the heartbroken.

I wonder what sadness I was trying to express by singing those songs?

I was nine years old, and apparently I was "all out of love."

We've all experienced times in childhood when parts of

ourselves felt exposed, when we needed someone to help us through something sad, terrible, or confusing. And these orphan parts of us end up lost, and we have no idea how to get anywhere in the world.

I believe that those orphaned parts of me were raised by immature older siblings, Approval and Admiration, who taught me I'd survive only if I could continually achieve enviable levels of success and admiration. I'd keep producing success because the alternative was to look inside myself, which would be terrifying. Approval and Admiration said I'd always need lots and lots of success and positive feedback to hide my very real insecurity.

They also gave me a very simple formula I needed to follow: Succeed at everything, be admired, keep achieving.

If you're familiar with the Enneagram,[1] you'll understand that as a 3, I'm very effective at getting things done and persuading people to go where I'm going. But it also means that when I feel as though I'm failing at what I'm doing, I think that I'm all out of love. More than that, I feel as though I'm disappearing.

All those things came tumbling out of my mouth years later as I sat with my friend Seth Haines while overlooking the overgrown willow trees in my backyard.

Seth is a Southern gentleman who lives in Arkansas. He's gentle and strong, tethered to something ancient and true. He and his wife, Amber, have four boys, the kind who bring home snakes and who conceal and carry Arkansas dirt in their pockets as if it were gold. Their life is busy and happy, filled with all the normal joy and anxiety packed into a family of six.

But when they almost lost their two-year-old son, Titus, Seth swallowed some dangerous glass.

Titus had been losing weight and was constantly sick, and they were worried. The only diagnosis they had was "failure to thrive," and the doctors didn't know what to prescribe. Titus's large eyes stared out at them as he began to slip away in the hospital.

When the doctors finally said, "All we can do is help him be as comfortable as possible," Seth decided he wasn't going to feel anything anymore. So he asked his sister to smuggle a bottle of gin into the hospital, and he started drinking in earnest. Gin was his alcohol of choice, perhaps because it was the choice of his father and grandfather before him.

When he was out with friends, family, and coworkers, he limited the number of drinks he would have, but in private, his daily regimen included polishing off a drink or two before he left his law offices and then drinking several more at home. This went on for a little more than a year, with Titus not getting any better, until Seth woke up one day with what he calls a "glorious Christian hangover."

That day was the beginning of his journey toward sobriety.

Seth wrote his story in a raw, gorgeous book called *Coming Clean: A Story of Faith*, which details the first ninety days of his sobriety. Seth's sin of choice was abusing alcohol, but as he says, "My alcoholism is not the thing, see. Neither is your eating disorder, your greed disorder, or your sex addiction.

Your sin is not the thing. The thing is under the sin. The thing is the pain. Sin management without redemption of life's pain is a losing proposition."[2]

So you can guess where Seth's questions focused when he and I talked, the time I couldn't hide under those willows.

If you're going to do the good work of restoring what's broken, you're going to have to deal with your own jagged glass and come out of hiding.

Where are you?

———

When the first human beings lost their way, God asked them a question. I find this hopeful. From the very first interaction, God was attentive and curious, inviting them to be honest.

> They heard the sound of the LORD God walking in
> the garden at the time of the evening breeze, and the
> man and his wife hid themselves from the presence
> of the LORD God among the trees of the garden. But
> the LORD God called to the man, and said to him,
> "Where are you?"   GENESIS 3:8-9

As the story goes in Genesis 3, this question comes directly after the first really big train wreck, after which things went hopelessly wrong. Whatever you believe about literal talking serpents and actual apples, this scene has been repeated so many times over the course of human history that it's obviously *more than* literal. It's true, in every desperate sense of the word.

The story of the first cover-up is the story of all the cover-ups, which we have reenacted many times. We could just as easily call these cover-ups *sin*, which is admittedly a grenade of a word, but let's be honest, what else would you call rape? What else would you call the slaughter that is happening right before our eyes at the hands of ISIS?

And what else would you call the small movement you make toward your coworker, who is not your spouse, following that undeniable spark? That small line you decidedly and intentionally cross? What else would you call it?

If you're still not convinced, what else would you call snarky Facebook comments?

I was recently speaking at my friend Andrew's church in Providence, Rhode Island, where I came across the best definition of sin I've ever heard: "Legitimate longings that have gone astray."

I have a legitimate longing to be significant, to see that whatever mark I make in my corner of the world *matters*. I have a legitimate longing for my words to find a soft place to land, in the hearts and minds of people who want to find a God who seems to be unfindable. I have a legitimate longing to be noticed and to be affirmed for what I bring to the world.

But the edge between using my gifts for the good of the world and relying on my gifts to make me valuable is razor-thin, and I fall off it entirely too often.

What do you do to get noticed? Where do your gifts blur

into self-indulgence? Where have your legitimate longings gone astray?

We can surely all agree that we have some idea of what *good* is but that we seem to be unable to carry it out consistently. And we have at least some idea of what *bad* is, and we seem to indulge in it more often than we'd like to admit.

There does seem to be an undeniable human propensity to mess things up, doesn't there?[3]

And when you mess things up, you feel shame, and so you run away and hide.

Sin first entered the picture when Adam and Eve mistrusted the one who had otherwise been trustworthy, because it suddenly seemed as if God might have been holding out on them. And so they reached out and grabbed the thing they believed should have been theirs in the first place (of course it was *they*; Adam was all too eager to get in on it with her but then conveniently offered Eve the blame). Then the blaming went back and forth until they were both covered in self-hatred. And then they heard God coming. That's when their innocence floated away.

And so they ran away and hid.

God pursued them with a question, one that brought them out of hiding.

"Where are you?" God asked.

Oh, God, where am I?

God hasn't stopped asking that question.

Where are you?

Before they chose to hide, Adam and Eve lived in the

7

Garden in the physical and emotional state of being naked and unashamed. To live naked and unashamed means to live in the radical vulnerability of complete trust. The closest resemblance we have now is a newborn baby with his or her mother.

We think growing up means getting increasingly more independent, but life in the Garden seemed to demonstrate something different: a vulnerability that involved both personal agency and dependence. Adam and Eve are instructed to take care of the Garden while also depending on the God who put them there in the first place. When we believed the lie that the serpent whispered to us, we lost the thread that connected personal agency to trust. And so every time we fail, we feel shame and go into hiding instead of looking back into the eyes of our mothers and receiving more of what we need to keep growing.

> God called to the Man: "Where are you?"
> He said, "I heard you in the garden and I was afraid because I was naked. And I hid."
> God said, "Who told you you were naked?"
> GENESIS 3:9-11, MSG

Adam evaded God's question. He told God that he had hidden, but he didn't tell God where he actually was. To admit out loud where we actually are is one of the most vulnerable things we can do. It's far easier to hide, even from ourselves. We hide because we are afraid.

When the serpent had come to the couple and incited

them out of that vulnerability and into mistrust, he also came with a question.

> The serpent was clever, more clever than any wild animal GOD had made. He spoke to the Woman: "Do I understand that God told you not to eat from any tree in the garden?" GENESIS 3:1, MSG

The word for "clever" (*arum*) can also mean "crafty or shrewd." The man and the woman had previously been naked but felt no shame. After their interaction with the crafty one, they *felt* naked. They were covered in shame for the very first time.

Have you ever met someone who had the uncanny ability of making you feel naked and ashamed?

When the serpent asked the woman if God had really told her not to eat from any tree in the Garden, he was planting a seed of doubt in her mind. The serpent was implying God could not be trusted.

Don't miss the larger truth happening here: Sin isn't the first true thing about being human. The first true thing about being human is living with God, and with one another, in the radical vulnerability of complete trust. And we gave that radical vulnerability away. We exchanged it for independence and mistrust and scarcity.

The work of restoration starts with the desire to come out of hiding and return to the radical vulnerability of complete trust.

Where are you? There are lots of places to hide when you feel exposed. We typically hide by fashioning armor that will cover our weaknesses and prevent us from having to be vulnerable.

Maybe you hide in your perfectionism.

Maybe you hide by deflecting praise.

Maybe you hide by always remaining the victim.

Maybe you hide by making sure you're always the first one to offer help but never being the one who needs help.

Maybe you hide by wearing the coat of the activist, but you won't admit that it's easier to love someone across the world than someone who lives in your own home.

Maybe you hide by insisting that you're a contemplative, but you won't admit that part of your lack of engagement is that you're just afraid.

Adam and Eve allowed God to *cover* them after they felt the hot shame of their nakedness (see Genesis 3:21). Do you dare to believe that your journey out of hiding will start with being clothed *by God*—not yourself—so that you can go where you need to go?

You've swallowed some jagged glass, and you've gone into hiding. This is part of what it means to be human. What would it take for you to come out of hiding? What would it take for you to name where you actually are? What would it feel like to return to a state of vulnerability and radical trust?

It's a wise person who knows where he or she is, even if hiding. It's from that honest place that wholeness can grow. For many of us, we're hiding in the very place where we lost our innocence, when we traded radical trust and vulnerability for shame and hiding. For some of you, this may have come from obvious trauma, and for others, it may have come from the minor cuts and bruises that accrued over time while you were growing up.

What sent you running? What made you hide?

I was in second grade, and I was shooting baskets alone at recess. Even back then, I liked to steal away by myself. I got nervous when Jimmy walked up to the basketball court and just stood there. Jimmy was the kind of kid who made you like him one moment and fear him the next. He asked to shoot baskets with me, and I asked him to leave, but he wouldn't. He just stood there and kept asking. I kept shooting, ignoring him. Finally, he rebounded one of my shots and got ahold of the ball, and when he did, something exploded inside of me. I tackled him and began punching him, over and over again.

In the principal's office, as she was trying to figure out what had happened, I couldn't stop crying. Jimmy sat there stone-faced, looking much stronger than I felt. Hot shame covered me as I cried and cried. Not only had I lost control of myself on the basketball court, but even worse, I was losing it in front of the person who intimidated me. Being exposed like that felt terrifying. This was the seventies; no crying was allowed if you wanted to be a strong boy. I never, ever wanted that to happen to me again.

I learned that day that I couldn't trust myself not to lose control—in anger or in sadness. And so I made a vow to hold it together, to never lose it, to keep those dangerous emotions inside of me.

It turns out that if you try to keep those dangerous emotions stuck inside of you, other things get stuck down there too.

I stuttered badly until I was about fourteen or fifteen. It's hard to describe what it's like to stutter, but back then no one called it a disability. Those of us who stutter are working really hard all the time, constantly searching for easier words that will replace the ones that get stuck in our throats. And the harder we work, the worse it gets.

My parents took me out of school one day to go to a speech therapist. We went to an old elementary school, in a storage room. Why didn't we meet at an office? Honestly, what were we doing in a storage room? I didn't want to be there, and I was convinced that it wasn't going to help. I really can't remember much about the therapy. What I remember in vivid detail was that some older boys were staring at me through the window in the door, making faces at me, making fun of me. I had never met them before, and I never saw them again, but something about their faces made me feel so exposed, so defective, that I never went back to speech therapy.

I learned that day that my voice was defective. And there was something about that storage room that said disabilities of any kind should be hidden, that they shouldn't be brought out to the light of day.

When you have a disability with your voice, you try to

make up for it by being spectacular in some other visible way. I chose sports.

I've always been a good athlete. I've made all-star and all-conference teams and have been named team captain many times. But it took me until I was in sixth grade to decide to play organized sports. I think I waited that long because I was nervous about how the other boys on the team would react to my stuttering. I couldn't wait for that first game. I remember putting on my uniform: white pants, black-and-gold shirt, and black hat with a gold *P* on it. We were the Pirates, and I was the starting shortstop and leadoff hitter.

I struck out in my first at bat.

Then I struck out in my second at bat.

And my third.

I prayed I wouldn't have a fourth-plate appearance, but I did.

And I struck out then, too.

So in my first game of organized baseball, I struck out four times.

I remember going home and lying on my bed, crying. My dad came in to talk to me, reassuring me that there would be other games and that we could work on my hitting. But I felt like such a failure. I imagined what it would be like to never get a hit, to never even touch the ball for the rest of the season.

Failure felt like the absolute worst thing in the world, and I must have made a vow then that I would work as hard as I could to never fail again.

I wouldn't know it until many years later, but I would grow

up to use my voice to discover strength in others. My voice would not be used to knock down people but instead to restore that which is broken, to set free that which is imprisoned.

Approval and Admiration played important roles in my life. They got me through some very scary times in childhood. They're not inherently bad. Everyone wants to be appreciated for his or her work in the world. But approval and admiration will take you only so far, and then they'll trap you there. I've hidden there for many, many years. I've worn that armor for too long.

My journey of restoration has been a long road of coming out of hiding to realize that I have a quiet but formidable strength, that my emotions are okay, and that my voice isn't broken. I'm learning to trust God and other people with my vulnerability instead of only my success.

I'm learning to answer God and others when asked where it is that I'm hiding. I'm learning to receive the clothes God has for me instead of insisting that I make them for myself. This is part of my journey out of hiding.

Where are you?

Mary and I recently performed a wedding for two close friends in Winter Park, Colorado. The ceremony was outside, in the thin air of nine thousand feet. Natalie and Chris wrote their own vows, using the Hebrew word *hineni*, which means "Here I am." It's used in the Scriptures in moments when God calls to someone when he or she is at a turning point, when God is calling that person on a journey. "*Hineni*" is the response people give to God when they want to indicate that they are all-in for the journey, even though they don't know where they are going. Natalie and Chris wanted to say "*hineni*" to each other, to communicate that the answer to the question "Where are you?" will *always* be "Here I am."

They gave me permission to reprint part of their vows:

I am very aware of my own flaws and ways I have
  and will miss the mark in loving you well.
When I am crazy about you . . . and when you make
  me crazy . . . Here I am.
When I want to run toward you . . . and when I want
  to run away . . . Here I am.
When our life is full of adventures . . . and when it's
  full of the mundane . . . Here I am.
When things go as we'd imagined them . . . and when
  they don't . . . Here I am.
I promise to learn with you,
to ask questions with you, to listen to you,
and to care for your heart, your body, and your soul.
From this moment forward, you have my wholehearted
  commitment.
There won't be anyone else.
You are the one I choose.
Here I am.

It was one of the most beautiful weddings I've ever been a part of.

"Abraham," God whispered one early morning, the chilly air feeling like razor blades around Abraham's shoulders. God was about to ask Abraham to sacrifice his only son on a distant mountain.

"*Hineni*," Abraham answered. Would Abraham trust God to provide, even if he had to give up what he loved most?

"Jacob," God whispered in a dream.

"*Hineni*," Jacob answered, his tongue sticking to the roof of his mouth. Would Jacob return to the land where he was from, to face his brother, whom he had deceived?

"Moses," God called out from the burning bush.

"*Hineni*," Moses answered, starting a conversation that would last for two chapters, finally ending with the decision to return to Egypt, the place from which he had hidden for forty years.

"*Hineni*" is the response you give God when you want to tell him that you're fully present and want to come out of hiding. You don't know where the journey will take you or even all that it will cost, but you want to say that you're fully present with God in a state of radical trust and vulnerability.

Is your heart fully present? Is your spirit fully present? Are you willing to walk toward vulnerability so that you can go on a journey of restoration? Or will you remain hidden? Will you come out of hiding and courageously name where you actually are so that you can begin the journey out of hiding—back into a life of vulnerability and trust? Richard Rohr wrote,

> Human strength admires holding on. Human weakness is about letting go into the Other, handing over the self to another and receiving your self from another. Human strength admires personal independence. But God's Mystery is total mutual dependence and interdependence. We like control more than surrender. God loves vulnerability. We admire needing no one. The Trinity is total intercommunion with all things and all being. We are practiced at hiding and protecting ourselves. God seems to be in some kind of total disclosure for the sake of creating and loving the other.[4]

"Steve," God calls out to me.

"*Hineni*," I answer. I don't know where this answer will take me, but I know I want to go, out of hiding and into trust.

Is God calling your name?

How will you answer?

Committing to your own restoration is risky. It might even feel selfish. But restoration is constructed by God to be *all-inclusive*. That's why *shalom* means "completeness, wholeness." True restoration for one person leads to restoration for another, or else it isn't restoration. We create a false bifurcation when we believe that the restoration of others is somehow different from our own restoration. We lose the plot if we believe that our own restoration is somehow less important than, or even separated from, the restoration of others.

Caring for your own restoration is essential if you're going to work for restoration in the world. If you don't commit to your own restoration, you'll continue to choose mistrust and violence as the only ways to deal with the brokenness you see inside of you and all around you.

Adam and Eve's sons will teach us that lesson, and it will be a costly one.

God will ask us *where we are* over and over again in our lives, because we'll get lost over and over again. At that moment, God isn't asking us to make a plan. God simply wants to call us out of hiding and into a new beginning.

May you hear God's voice calling your name
in your deepest, darkest corner of shame, where
you have hidden yourself away from everybody,
even yourself. And may you rise from that
place and boldly answer, "Here I am."

QUESTIONS *for Reflection & Discussion*

1. In what ways can you relate to the stories from Steve's childhood? What is one story from your own childhood that marked you in a similar way?

2. Steve said immature siblings named Approval and Admiration raised him. What words would describe how you tried to gain a sense of identity and safety for yourself?

3. Finish this sentence and explain your answer: Vulnerability is _____.

4. Where are you with God in terms of wanting to be fully present and wanting to come out of hiding?

5. If God asked you, "Where are you?" right now, how would you answer if you knew you were completely safe in answering with whatever was really true?

-2-

AM I MY BROTHER'S
KEEPER?

Copernicus discovered that Earth is not the center of the universe.
Now we have to discover that we are not the center of any universe either.

RICHARD ROHR,
Mature Spirituality, AUGUST 29, 2016

THE SUN HAD pounded him into powder by midday, so
he rested in the shade. He didn't remember falling asleep,
but the same dream that always haunted him returned. He
saw a field with long, straight rows containing seeds that he
knew would never sprout. And then the question came, as it
always did. He screamed as his eyes shot open. He shivered
as though night had fallen, but the cool evening breeze was
still a long way off.

Many years had passed since he first heard the question—
after he had lured his brother, Abel, to a field and murdered
him, watching Abel's blood cover his hands and pool around
his feet. Cain buried Abel in the same field where Abel had

tended his flocks, a lush meadow hidden beside a trickling stream.

"Where is your brother?" God had asked him (see Genesis 4:9).

Cain winced as he remembered his answer, which he had also tried to bury, but like his recurring nightmare, it didn't stay buried because something deep within wouldn't allow it.

"I don't know," he had replied. "Am I my brother's keeper?"

God never answered Cain's question.

When a question like this is raised in the Scriptures and there's no answer, a long conversation about it will take place, one that spans many generations, many stories, and much conflict. This is comforting in an odd way, isn't it? When a brother murders a brother, even in the Bible, we can't expect that it will be resolved in a single conversation.

Cain worked the soil, growing fruits, grains, and vegetables. Abel tended sheep. When it came time to bring sacrifices to God, Cain brought "some of the fruits of the soil" as an offering (verse 3, NIV). Abel, on the other hand, brought "fat portions from some of the firstborn of his flock" (verse 4, NIV). God considered both offerings and approved of Abel's but not Cain's.

Why? This seems capricious. Is this how God will treat people from now on?

There's some debate about why God rejected Cain's offering while accepting Abel's. It seems unlikely that it was about fruits and vegetables versus meat. God seemed to see something in Cain's offering that was different from Abel's.

Interestingly, the name *Cain* is related to a verb meaning "to possess" or "to gain," while *Abel* means "breath," "vapor," or "gentle breeze." What does it mean that the need to possess can choke out breath? What does it mean that the need to gain something will sometimes overpower those who are gentle?

When Abel chose to give God the fat from his firstborn sheep, he gave God something that was very close to his heart. Abel most likely came to love his sheep, especially the firstborn. Abel was giving God his best—the really good stuff—but I think there's more to this story than just sheep.

Abel was also giving God something *intimate*. When Cain chose to give God *some* of the produce that he grew, he was withholding something, mistrusting God and trusting instead in the produce to provide what was needed. He was more concerned with gaining and possessing, so he gave a lesser gift.

Cain hid, while Abel risked the more vulnerable option of trusting.

What do you seek to possess or acquire that keeps you from intimacy? Where do you withhold your best—the really good stuff—because of your need to keep gaining more?

If you're a perfectionist, you're locking away the really good stuff until you're sure no one will reject it. You're attempting to gain more control.

If you're a workaholic, you have convinced yourself that it's okay that your kids don't get the really good stuff from you because they'll be taken care of financially. You're attempting to gain more money.

If you're addicted to approval, you've hidden your true self so well that you can't find it anymore. As more people *like* you, you realize that fewer people *love* you because you've never given them anything real to love.

The particular story of Cain and Abel becomes universal when you realize that you can kill off the gentle breeze of intimacy by attempting to possess more while you give less.

I actually feel some empathy for Cain. When you start down the road of acquiring and possessing, it's hard to turn back. In my attempts to acquire and possess admiration, I have sometimes traded being known and loved for being consumed and admired. It's easier to write a blog post that gets hundreds of likes on Facebook than it is to risk rejection by saying the hard but true (and private) thing to someone with whom I live or work. But as I hold that emotion and turn it around for a while, an invitation shows up.

Will I risk rejection so that someone else might be made whole?

I get Cain. My desire to succeed, to win approval and admiration, feels a lot like possession. But it's hard to be your brother's keeper when your chief concern is being more successful than your brother.

When I learned to hide my disabilities, my strong emotions, and my real voice, I learned to gain success by showing how strong I was, how in control I was, how I could adapt my voice to fit whatever was needed, even if it wasn't even really my voice. I've learned to look after my own success, hedging my bets and hiding my true self because it might appear weak or out of control.

Am I my brother's keeper? is a defensive question, designed to ensure that the one who asks it can remain in hiding. It's cloaked in deceit. Cain murdered Abel, and God knew it. Cain was lying to God, but he may have even been lying to himself, unable to even see the length to which he had gone in order to gain, or acquire, for himself.

This story of the first brothers—and this word *keeper*—is the beginning of an arc that shoots all the way through the Hebrew Scriptures and the New Testament. I need to spend a few paragraphs building the foundation of that arc so that you can see how far it goes. In chapter 3, I will describe how that arc continues and where it eventually goes. Interestingly, it involves another set of brothers who are asking the exact same question (*Am I my brother's keeper?*).

The word translated as "keeper" is a substantive form of the Hebrew word *shamar*, which means "to keep, guard, watch over, tend, or save a life."

The first usage of *shamar* is found in Genesis 2:15: "The LORD God took the man and put him in the garden of Eden to till it and keep [*shamar*] it."

The word translated as "put" is less like a chess move and more like a loving gardener planting a prized flower in just the right spot. The word translated as "put" is a form of the verb *yanach*, which means "to cause to rest, settle down, remain."

We might paraphrase Genesis 2:15 like this:

God caused the humans to be settled into the garden, where they would rest and remain. Out of that resting and remaining, they would cultivate the life that grew around them, and they would tend to that life and guard it so it would flourish.

Cain and Abel had the unenviable task of trying to cultivate the life that was growing around them *outside* of the Garden. It was hard work, and no one had tried it before. It's always hard to go first.

Cain's sin, I think, is that he was convinced he was playing a zero-sum game. If he gave away his best—the really good stuff—there wouldn't be anything left to sustain him. He believed that he had to make a choice: guard his own future or guard his brother. So he guarded his future instead of his brother's.

Where are you, Cain? You can't guard anything when you're hiding.

You will guard many things in your life. Some of what you guard will cause you and others to flourish, and some of what you guard will kill off the good life that is growing in you and in others.

Am I my brother's keeper? is a question asked by someone who believes in the law of scarcity: There's not enough to go around, so you need to make sure you keep enough for yourself.

Have you ever ordered pizza for three people and then inwardly freaked out when you realized that you might be the person who gets only two slices? You're polite enough not to grab three pieces right away, but you want to.

Many years ago, Mary and I were looking for a couch, and we ended up at a large outlet store. We were told what to do by some friends who had been there before.

"Get there early because there's going to be a huge line. Then, when the doors open, *run* to the back where the couches are and immediately sit on the one you like. But you're going to have to be quick and really know what you want because usually there are only a few deals."

So we ran and immediately sat on a large gray sectional couch that was 75 percent off. We bought it but never loved it. We ended up giving it away a few years later.

It's a funny story until you realize that those are the same rules most of us live by in far more important matters than choosing couches.

If you believe that life is a zero-sum game, you'll work hard at acquiring enough for yourself, holding back your best for sometime in the future, when there's enough to go around. There is something terrifying about giving your best to God when you don't know how you'll get what you need.

And let's be honest: Abel gave God his best and he was murdered.

I wonder if we resist guarding our brother because it feels a lot like dying.

Actually, I don't wonder about it, because it happened to me. My hunger to acquire almost choked out a gentle breeze.

———

Only a table separated us on that muggy summer day as we sat outside at a café, but we were a million miles apart. We were both so frustrated, feeling misunderstood and stuck. It's a good thing we were sitting outside, because we were yelling. We had gotten to the place where we believed the worst about each other.

Steve has piercing blue eyes; a soft, vulnerable heart; and truckloads of passion. A year earlier, he had joined our church, Genesis, as the associate pastor. When he plays the piano and sings, it's with so much passion that a vein pops out on his forehead. Steve will drop anything to help anyone; his outsized heart breaks for those in need. He's a pastor in every sense of the word, and relationships are the most important thing in the world to him.

And yet something wasn't working between us. When we met for our weekly meetings, a growing tension developed that took a long time to name. When I asked him about it, he told me I was making decisions that he wouldn't have made. As a first-year church planter, I felt threatened by this. I didn't have the humility to consider that maybe he was right, so I held him at a distance. I was choosing to withhold my best—the really good stuff—because I didn't trust him. This made him question himself and the job he was doing.

The truth? I felt judged by Steve, and I didn't know what to do about it. That's why I held him at a distance. It's why I wasn't including him in decisions anymore. I was withholding my best from him because I didn't know if anything would be left if I gave him my best. I was guarding *my* future, worried about my own success and unable to see that I was back on the basketball court, feeling intimidated and scared.

This went on for months. We tried discussing it, but we both felt emotionally drained by the situation. We brought in someone from our denomination to help, but we still couldn't see or hear each other. I remember thinking that I didn't need this conflict or this emotional weight. Church planting was hard enough.

I felt like a failure when I was around Steve. I kept having conversations with him in my mind, finally saying things clearly that I felt I had botched with him in person. When I thought about him, the knots inside of me kept tightening, squeezing compassion out and fortifying my sense of entitlement.

And then one Friday he called me to apologize for the ways he had hurt me. He said he knew working with him was confusing and difficult. And then he said, "Steve, I'm convinced that the person you see is not the person who I actually am. And I'm begging you to give me another chance."

Steve, God was calling out to me. It was a *hineni* moment. Was I willing to show up and be vulnerable? Was I willing to be fully present with my heart and my spirit?

Something changed inside of me after that phone call. The next day, I went on a long run by myself. I like running alone because it provides some time and space to think and breathe. About a third of the way into the run, I remembered a walk that Mary and I had taken years before, when Mary mustered up the strength to ask me a question that had been haunting her for years.

"For a very long time," she said, "I have felt like you treat me as if I'm what's wrong with this relationship. And I need to know if that's true, or if I'm crazy." That was a huge moment for our marriage, when I realized that I'd been hurting Mary for years. I wrote about it in my first book, *Beginnings: The First Seven Days of the Rest of Your Life*. It was so hard to admit that she was right.

On that run, I heard God's voice, very gently but unmistakably saying, "Do you think it's possible that's how you're treating Steve?"

The pain of its truth shot through my body. I had seen Steve as an impediment to my pastoring Genesis, but instead, he was teaching me how to do it.

My heart broke wide open, and I saw the ways in which I had hurt him and the ways it was confusing for him to work with me.

The following Tuesday we had a meeting scheduled with our mutual friend Matt, one of the kindest men I know. He's one of Steve's closest friends, so I asked him to try to help me really see Steve. Steve and I sat across from each other at a different table this time, at a different restaurant, and I asked if I could open the conversation. I looked right at Steve, and I told him about what happened on my run. I told him I was so sorry for how I'd treated him as though he were the problem. I listed some specific ways I saw how he was trying to make our relationship work. I told him I, too, wanted to make it work.

Steve was gracious. We talked and talked about what making it work would mean, and Matt was so helpful. We knew we still had to work through issues that wouldn't magically disappear, so we made a plan for how to work through those moving forward. At the end of that long conversation, we both felt as though a new way had been made. We forgave each other. We agreed that we wanted to believe the best about each other and that we wanted to try to make it work. It was a miracle.

That was two years ago, and our relationship is now strong and growing stronger. We're still very different, and sometimes we have to work hard to understand each other, but there's mutual trust. It's a gift to work with Steve; he's such a huge part of who Genesis is as a church.

And I'm no longer withholding the really good stuff from him.

When you're honest about where you are, and when you choose trust instead of mistrust, you will be given the opportunity to test it out on another human being—your brother or sister. Trust isn't a concept. It's a way of being in relationship in which you seek mutual flourishing.

Something is wrong if your own flourishing is dependent on your brother not flourishing. When you're stressed and in conflict, you tend to believe that by eliminating the other person, you will eliminate the jagged piece of glass that you've swallowed. You're back on the basketball court, pounding the other person until he or she disappears. If you keep doing that, your sense of entitlement will keep growing, while your own sense of contentment and joy will keep diminishing. That is the universal warning that the story of Cain and Abel offers.

This is the primary lesson I learned with Steve: My task as the pastor of this church is to cultivate the life that is growing around me, guarding it so that it flourishes. Instead of tending to Steve's life, I felt threatened by him. I saw him as an enemy who was too big for me, who was going to devour me. But on that long run, God gently placed me back in the Garden, causing me to rest and to remember my work: to see the sacred future and guard it. Steve wasn't the enemy. He was a human being whose flourishing was connected to my own flourishing. It just took me a long time to see it.

The paradoxical truth I'm learning is that a gentle breeze can eventually drive off the need to gain more. But it takes time.

My work is not to gain more admiration and approval. And your work is not to gain more control and more order for you to be okay, or to gain more safety and security before making big life decisions.

Your work, and my work, is to see to the sacred future and to tend to it. And you can't do that if you're caught in a zero-sum game in which you try to gain more—of whatever it is you're trying to gain—for yourself. And yet I seem to have a program installed in my hard drive that keeps me working to gain approval instead of choosing to give my best: the really good stuff—intimacy.

———•———

What help do you need for healing? What hope do you need so that you can move forward and share that healing with others? What do you need to say to God to be restored?

> Cain said to the LORD, "My punishment is greater than I can bear! Today you have driven me away from the soil, and I shall be hidden from your face; I shall be a fugitive and a wanderer on the earth, and anyone who meets me may kill me."

God answered Cain's cry with mercy.

> Then the LORD said to him, "Not so! Whoever kills Cain will suffer a sevenfold vengeance." And the LORD put a mark on Cain, so that no one who came upon him would kill him. Then Cain went away from the presence of the LORD, and settled in the land of Nod, east of Eden.   GENESIS 4:13-16

God marked Cain, protecting him so that he would live. And he lived a long time, but we have no record that he turned back to God. Instead, after being protected by God with this mysterious mark, Cain "went away from the presence of the Lord, and settled in the land of Nod, east of Eden" (verse 16).

Why didn't he turn toward God after such an act of mercy? Why did he allow his shame to speak louder than God's mark of protection? The verb translated "went away" is from the Hebrew word *yatsa*, meaning "to go forth, exit." He exited from the *paneh*, literally "face," of God.

When shame wins, we feel as though we can no longer look into the face of God.

One of the most courageous things you will ever do is to turn away from shame and return to the face of God, where you will find oceans of mercy.

And then you'll be *sent* somewhere, which is a very different thing than going away on your own.

Unfortunately, the law of scarcity runs roughshod over Western culture, especially over our religious and political institutions. The blood of Abel calls to us from the grave, asking us to believe that we can trust God to give us the really good stuff, over and over again, especially when we give our best away. It calls to us to be a gentle breeze that offers relief instead of being people who clamor for more and more gain.

May you have the courage to give God your
really good stuff, believing that you can trust
God completely with your life and with your
future, so that at all times, in all things, you may
flourish, causing life to grow all around you.

QUESTIONS *for Reflection & Discussion*

1. Do you have a story similar to the one the author shares about the associate pastor, Steve, in which trust was broken? What happened?

2. What type of environment do you thrive in, allowing you to cultivate the life that grows around you, tend to that life, and guard it so that it flourishes?

3. How do you "guard" your brother and sister without becoming codependent or doing their work for them?

4. Have you ever run away from God's face? If so, how was the voice of shame involved in your decision to run?

5. How do we differentiate between needed self-care and the seeking of gain?

WHAT ARE YOU SEEKING?

Though your destination is not yet clear
You can trust the promise of this opening;
Unfurl yourself into the grace of beginning
That is at one with your life's desire.

JOHN O'DONOHUE,
"FOR A NEW BEGINNING"

HIS PATCHY BEARD was embarrassing.

He was only seventeen, and he was anxious to grow into his man body. He was lithe, even slight, unlike his older brothers, who had rocks for hands and thick, lustrous beards. Still, the girls lingered over him as he ambled by, barely able to hide their hunger for him. He was irresistible—to everyone except his brothers.

His name is Joseph. The date is 1898 BC. The place is the Land of Canaan.

His brothers had grown weary of his posturing. His charisma and penchant for self-aggrandizement only made them hate him more. Their hatred for him was venomous, fueled in part because they knew that their father, Jacob, loved Joseph most. Joseph was the son of Rachel, the woman Jacob loved. Jacob didn't love their mother, Leah, with her milky eyes and big bones. Most of her teeth were gone by this time; she had given up. She passed on her venom to them, whispering and sighing about *that boy.*

In Genesis 37:4, we read, "When his brothers realized that their father loved him more than them, they grew to hate him—they wouldn't even speak to him" (MSG). This story continues the arc of one of the major themes of Scripture, building on the foundation that was laid in the last chapter, when a brother didn't believe that he was his brother's keeper. Only this time, the brothers are the twelve sons of Israel.

In the Hebrew, the last word in Genesis 37:4 is *shalom.* Joseph's brothers hated him so much that they could not speak to him with shalom. They could not be their brother's keeper.

One day, Jacob decided to send Joseph to check on his brothers, who were watching the family sheep. One of the words the writer used is fascinating.

> He said to him, "Go now, see if it is well with your brothers and with the flock; and bring word back to me." So he sent him from the valley of Hebron.
>
> GENESIS 37:14

Hebron is the name of an actual place from which Jacob sent Joseph, but it also means "association." It comes from the word *heber*, which means "shared association, society." Joseph is being sent away from a society where he is known, into the unknown, to find his brothers, who hate him.

Thanks, Dad.

To "see if it is *well* with your brothers" means to "see to the shalom of your brothers." In the last story of Genesis, a book filled with violence and conflict between brothers, a son is sent out by his father to see to the shalom of his brothers, to gather up all the broken pieces of brotherhood and fashion together a mosaic of wholeness. It's a staggering story of restoration.

The seventeen-year-old with the patchy beard set out into the dusty wilderness, his mouth chalky from the heat and also from fear. He knew his brothers hated him. And so he straightened his spine under the blistering sun, believing that it just might ease the trembling. He walked and walked, mile after lonely mile, but those brothers of his were nowhere to be found. But still he kept walking.

Finally at dusk, when fingers of hunger pressed into his thin belly, he came upon a short man with wispy white hair. His burly forearms told stories of strength, but his eyes were shifty. He was borne by an ancient donkey that appeared to be blind in one eye (but it could have been a scowl). The donkey had sparse fur, barely covering its bony frame.

"What are you seeking?" the man barked, blinking against the sun's dying rays and not liking what he saw. His question rang like a gunshot across the empty fields.

"I am seeking my brothers," Joseph whispered, as if all at once he understood the task his father had given him.

Finally in Genesis, a brother isn't escaping a brother. A brother isn't deceiving a brother. A brother isn't murdering a brother. A brother is *seeking* his brothers. A brother is working for restoration. A brother is *seeing to the work of shalom.* *Genesis* means "beginning." It's significant that the "beginning" of the story of God's people ends with a brother being sent into harm's way by his father to see to the shalom of his brothers. When you're dealing with an arc this expansive, *this* story almost always has to do with *that one.*

Immediately, Joseph began to back away from the stranger, but not before the man's question lodged deep within his psyche. Before he knew it, he was running across the rocks, away from everything he'd ever known. The boy with the patchy beard was about to leave on a journey to see to the shalom of not only his brothers but also the whole world.

It would lead him into slavery. It would lead him into being falsely accused and thrown in jail. It would lead him away from his family for untold years. And it would lead him into providing food for a country that was starving. Because he started out by seeking the shalom of his brothers, he ended up seeking the shalom of the entire world.

What are *you* seeking?

Don't answer too soon. Let your life answer the question before you answer what you'd *like* to be seeking. When you look at your life—the one you actually have and the decisions you've actually made—what does it tell you that you *are* seeking?

———

My friend Catie is vivacious, honest, and sparkling with empathy. Before becoming a mother, she worked full-time as a lawyer. But before any of that, she was a child who didn't have a real friend for the first thirteen years of her life. She was bullied, isolated, and shamed by her peers at school. Every day. All day long.

Outside the safe walls of her home and family, no one was seeing to her shalom.

To cope with the pain of being different, she made herself a chameleon, being whatever she thought people wanted her to be. Empty and hollow from her efforts, Catie felt the black dog of depression growling and snarling, trapping her in a corner of herself. Emotions were pain, so she cut herself off from having them at all.

Despite her family's efforts to keep her going, the darkness often got too dark. Soon she became enslaved to self-loathing. She hid there for a very long time. That's where she was when I first met her. I just didn't know it.

"For as long as I can remember, I've been consumed with loneliness and fear," she told me.

Catie never felt lonely or afraid around her dad, Russ. He was her hero and a safe place. When all the world seemed to reject her, Catie's dad loved her back from the edge many times.

And then Russ got cancer.

When his skin turned yellow and it became clear that he

wasn't going to make it much longer, I asked Catie how she was preparing to live without her dad.

"Well, he's had cancer for three years, so we've had time to process it," she told me. "I'm sure I'll be sad, but it'll be fine."

I think she really meant it. Still disconnected from emotion, she believed that because she *knew* he was going to die, she would be protected from the pain, that somehow knowledge would save her. Feelings certainly wouldn't.

Catie gave the eulogy at her father's funeral. Russ was a photographer for a news station, and his travels had taken him all around the world. Everybody at the news station talked about Russ the way Catie did: He was larger than life, and they all loved him. The thing that struck me most about Catie's eulogy was how well she seemed to be taking her dad's death. It was surprising, and it seemed like a gift from God.

Catie had come on staff at Genesis a few months before her dad died, and she quickly became the person who held our church together operationally. She loves details, whereas I see details as distractions from the really important things. She sees the world in systems, whereas I see it in blank canvases. Catie has the rare gift of being able to see both the big picture and the pixels from which it's made.

She loves me and believes in me, and she fights to make sure I'm spending my time doing those things that only I can do. She says God told her she was supposed to help us plant the church, and I believe her. I can't imagine Genesis, or my own place within it, without Catie.

But soon after her dad died, Catie began to unravel.

The pain of her dad's death eventually consumed her. Out of habit she covered it up pretty well, most of the time. But it all came crashing down in April 2015, and by May, Catie was in her psychiatrist's office, unable to function. Her psychiatrist asked if she could commit to her own safety until their next appointment.

Where are you? Catie was being asked, in about a thousand ways.

Catie looked her psychiatrist in the eye and told her she felt certain she should no longer be alive. She was sure her husband and son would be better off without her. The pain and loneliness had finally become too much.

Catie was admitted to the hospital that evening.

Mary and I were on vacation in Florida when all of this was happening. When Catie called me, I was sitting in the airport in Fort Myers. She told me she was going to need time off work, indefinitely, and that she had been hospitalized because she wanted to harm herself. She was trying so hard to hold it together, this person who holds everything and everyone else together. It was so hard for her to tell me she couldn't do it anymore. She didn't want to let me down.

But somehow she knew that if she had any hope of being whole, she was going to have to risk letting me down.

I listened. I asked questions. I affirmed her choice to pursue her own healing and recovery. I told her Genesis was going to be okay. I told her I believed she was going to be okay. Honestly, I did believe that, but I was freaking out, too. The spirit of scarcity was creeping in. I had no idea how to do Genesis without Catie. But then I felt bad for thinking about Genesis at all.

Catie was in the hospital for almost a week. When she was released, she was no longer in danger of taking her life, but she was shaky, unsure of herself and of everyone else. The first time we got together after she left the hospital, she was quiet and hesitant, but she was present (she would want me to tell you that she was on quite a lot of medication at that particular point in time).

I knew from that moment that Catie was going to make it. Instead of hiding from her pain or masking it, she chose to face it with vulnerability. It's one of the most courageous things I've ever witnessed. Hiding is lonely, but it's far easier than being vulnerable.

"*Hineni*," Catie was whispering. She didn't know where this journey would take her. But she knew she wanted to go on the journey rather than end it.

She finally got a glimpse of what she was seeking.

That was a little more than two years ago. Catie has since been through a nine-month intensive outpatient therapy program that helped to resize the voices of shame and fear. She has a much healthier relationship with herself, with her family and friends, and with her work. She organized a church community group that meets at her house, and she cooks meals for people in our church who are going through challenging times, have just had a baby, or are just not doing very well. She shares her story with anyone who asks and feels called to help others walk the path she walked.

This is how wholeness works: What has been broken and restored in you and me is being transformed into healing for the rest of the world.

These days, Catie is in the midst of a discernment process about moving into a new vocation: walking alongside those in deep emotional pain. I affirm her call. She is moving toward wholeness, and it's like watching a sunrise.

Vulnerability is a fragrance, more than anything. It starts with an intentionality to come out of hiding and face down whatever it is that needs to be faced down. It's fragile: You can't force someone—or yourself—to be vulnerable. But you begin to smell its fragrance when you're around someone like Catie. She is seeing to the shalom of her brothers and sisters. She is becoming vulnerable, for her own sake and for the sake of our church. She is seeking wholeness.

What are you seeking?

———⋅———

After Joseph found his brothers, they planned to kill him. They stripped him of his robe and dropped him into a cistern, then changed their minds about leaving him to die. Instead, they sold him to a band of slave traders. Joseph was later sold to the Egyptians, and soon afterward he was thrown into prison after being falsely accused of sleeping with his boss's wife.

It's unclear how long Joseph was in prison; it could have been as short as two years or as long as twelve. When he finally got out of prison after interpreting Pharaoh's dream, he was put in charge of all of Egypt, second only to Pharaoh.

After interpreting that dream, which foretold seven years of abundance followed by seven years of famine, Joseph engineered a strategy for saving enough grain to survive the years of famine. And during that time, he never saw his beloved father, never saw his brothers, and lived in exile, away from his *hebron*, his known society. There is no record of God speaking to Joseph at any time during his long story.

And yet we read in Genesis 39:21 that "the LORD was with Joseph and showed him steadfast love." When Joseph experienced all those years of hardship sustained by the steadfast love of God, humility must have grown in him.

At the end of Genesis, Joseph meets with his brothers, offering them the gentle breeze of forgiveness as well as a new *hebron*, where they would not starve, in which to live and raise their families. Through it all, he was seeing to the shalom of his brothers. He became *humble*, for his own sake and for the sake of the world. He was seeking wholeness.

What is growing in you? What are you becoming, not only for your own sake but also for the sake of the world?

My friends Rich and Rebecca have two children, a boy and a girl. When those kids were still very young, ages six and four, Rich was traveling a lot for work, spending about two hundred nights a year on the road. He hated it, but this job was supporting his family and paying their mortgage. So he kept working and traveling and hoping things would change someday.

One morning, his four-year-old daughter was sitting on Rich's lap, and she asked him a question.

"Where do you live, Daddy?"

"I live here, silly," Rich told her.

"Then why are you never here?"

Her question was a bullet; it went straight in and stopped his heart. He broke down and wept. He wasn't around enough for her to know that he even *lived* there. That initiated some hard conversations between Rich and Rebecca, which led to a job change. Now Rich's daughter doesn't wonder where her daddy lives anymore. Rich is seeing to the shalom of his family. He is creating a *family*, for his own sake and for the sake of the world. He is seeking wholeness.

My friend Kara is a mother of four and an artist. Her funky blue glasses cover dark, deep eyes that hold beauty and pain. She recently preached at our church, and she started with this courageous sentence: "My name is Kara . . . and I really want to be significant. In the world, in my home. That fear of 'not enough' has driven me to a place of practicality and 'should' that has squashed creativity and beauty in my life."

Recently, Kara decided that she needed to let art back into her life. She needs to create, to spin color and words and paper and freedom, for her own enjoyment and for the good of the world.

Kara finished her sermon this way:

What is happening is not just the beauty of art
being created, but the unfolding beauty of myself,

which will breathe life into others. . . . While
I still hope I get to create things and inspire others
to create, around the world maybe even, I am
confident of this: that my God loves me and that
he cares deeply not only about my needs but also
about my desires. And that he gave me a gift to
share to remind others of the goodness of our God,
even in the darkest hours. So because I love God
and because art is a way that I get to experience
and commune with him, I desire to make it a
more permanent part of my life. It is vulnerable
because it touches on really deep parts of my
soul that are scary to share. And yet it is worth it,
because often those deepest parts are what need
to be touched—in myself and in others. And so
here I am, Kara Groff, creative see-er of beauty,
and significant—even if just in the everyday small
moments, discovering who God created me to be
and delighting in that.[1]

Kara is seeing to the shalom of her brothers and sisters.
She is becoming *significant*, for her own sake and for the sake
of the world. She is seeking wholeness.

My friends Belinda Bauman and Lynne Hybels, along
with twelve other women, climbed Mount Kilimanjaro
in March 2016, summiting on March 8, which was
International Women's Day. They climbed for women such
as Esperance, who lives in the Democratic Republic of the

Congo. Esperance watched her husband die at the hand of rebels. She was violently raped and would have died if her sisters hadn't rescued her. Across a blank sheet of paper, Esperance, who can't read or write, had someone write the words: "Tell the world." Then she stamped her thumbprint underneath.

"Tell them my story," Esperance whispered.

Belinda Bauman couldn't get Esperance's voice out of her head, and the result was that she founded One Million Thumbprints, a grassroots campaign seeking to catalyze a groundswell of people focused on overcoming the effects of war upon women through storytelling, advocacy, and fundraising. Belinda and Lynne are seeing to the shalom of their brothers and sisters. They are becoming *advocates*, for their own sake and for the sake of some of the poorest women in the world. They are seeking wholeness.

My friend Matt Bays wrote a hauntingly hopeful book called *Finding God in the Ruins*, in which he tells his story of being sexually abused by his older brother, who was being sexually abused by their stepfather, a monster of a man who devastated their home with violence for more than ten years.[2] Matt is a force of joy, a boundless source of creativity and hope. He wrote about the healing and wholeness that comes not by erasing your pain but by meeting God in that pain and being known as God's beloved. Matt is seeing to the shalom of his brothers and sisters. He is becoming *hopeful*, for his own sake and for the sake of the world. He is seeking wholeness.

———•———

So how do you figure out what you're supposed to be seeking?

In my experience, what you need to seek comes disguised in your own pain, and you'll see it if you are paying attention. It also comes disguised as your *Sehnsucht* (that elusive thing you ardently long for but seems unattainable). It may even come hidden somewhere underneath that thing you are chasing with the energy of Cain, that thing you can't get enough of but isn't nearly enough. Joseph wanted fame, and he got it, but it wasn't what he thought it was going to be or with whom he wanted it.

And of course there's a way in which our sin can reveal the calling written on our souls, if we follow it all the way through. This is the hidden grace of God: Sometimes our true secrets—the ones we need to tell in order to change the world—are revealed by a catastrophic fall or devastating disappointment.

For some of us, even our limits can reveal the really good stuff inside of us that is there for the sake of the world.

I know a woman in her late seventies who has had chronic health problems for years. In the last five years or so, they have intensified. She won't be climbing any mountain anytime soon. She won't be painting or writing books or volunteering at church.

But she prays.

She prays and prays and prays all day. She prays for healing for everyone and everything she can think of. She is small in stature—she might be five feet tall—but she is mighty in spirit.

What are you seeking?

Maybe it's the reconciliation that needs to replace the racism in your community.

Maybe it's healing for those who are sick and suffering.

Maybe it's the little boy on the autism spectrum who needs you next to him.

Maybe it's the book that needs to be written.

Maybe it's the well that needs to be dug so that children have access to clean water.

Maybe it's slowing down so that you can be present.

Maybe it's the song that needs to be composed.

Maybe it's the forgiveness that needs to be offered.

Maybe it's the forgiveness that needs to be received.

Maybe it's prayer.

Maybe it's rest.

Whatever it is that you're seeking, it's connected to your secret—how you specifically want to change the world—and it needs to be shared. When you begin to awaken to the really good stuff that's in you, and when you begin to realize that it's there to be shared, you are seeking wholeness. When you keep pressing in, even though sharing it threatens to scare you right back into hiding, you are seeking wholeness.

And when it begins to become clear that your life really is showing you what you are seeking, then it's time to discover where it is you are *going*.

May you begin to awaken to the really good
stuff that is inside of you, and may you have
the courage to share it, for your own soul's
sake and for the sake of the world.

QUESTIONS *for Reflection & Discussion*

1. Have you ever experienced the gift of someone else seeing to *your* shalom? What happened, and how did it affect you?

2. Where do you see brokenness that breaks your heart? Where do you see alienation that makes you work for reconciliation? Where do you see the pieces of jagged glass wedged where nobody else seems to?

3. In what ways are you seeing to the shalom of your brothers and sisters right now? How is that affecting you and those around you?

4. Are you ready to say "*hineni*" to God (your heart is fully present and you're ready to come out of hiding to see to the shalom of your brothers and sisters)? What is your next step?

5. What is one thing you might need to consider stopping or putting on hold so that you can have space, time, and energy to see to the shalom of someone else?

— 4 —

WHERE ARE YOU
GOING?

It's a dangerous business, Frodo, going out of your door. . . .
You step into the Road, and if you don't keep your feet,
there is no knowing where you might be swept off to.

BILBO BAGGINS
IN *The Fellowship of the Ring*

A FEW YEARS AGO, a long-held dream shattered in pieces all around me, and something inside of me died. Out of that death came an invitation to something bright and brand new, but it took a while to see it.

It turns out that dreams are sturdy and stubborn things.

Dreams are all about where you are going. But it takes a wise person to know if your dream calls you to where you need to go or if it's a distraction from where you need to go.

Until the spring of 2014, I was the associate pastor at a church I had loved for a very long time. The senior pastor (Dave) and I grew very close. We often sat on his front

porch and talked about the future. He has seen to my shalom in very meaningful ways. It was an unbelievable honor
for me to be able to see to the shalom of this church—his
church—together.

I'd been listening to his sermons for twenty years, first
on tape, then CD, and finally in person. It was from him I
learned how to ask questions about the Bible, how to become
an archaeologist of those words and those stories, and how to
uncover the God of amazing grace. He was the first preacher
who helped me see underneath and around the perplexing
stories found in the Scriptures.

My dream was to be the next senior pastor at this church,
and it almost happened. It felt as though I had been preparing for this promotion my whole life. I was certain that God
was leading me into it.

"I dream of the day," Dave told me more than once,
"when I walk across the gathering place and I hear people
whispering that you're *better* than I am. If you weren't a son,
you would feel threatening to me," he said. "But because you
are a son, I can't wait for that day to come."

I believe that he meant it, with all his heart, and I drank
those words in. I idolized him for years; I patterned my
preaching after his when I was young. I couldn't think of
anything in my career that I wanted more than to follow him
as the next senior pastor at this church.

But things went wrong. I love the people of this church
to this day, and I love Dave, and I believe that they love me.
And we honestly all did the best we knew how to do. But

navigating a succession plan is a minefield of potential problems, and we stepped on quite a few of them.

I'm an activator—I see things that need to happen, and I
make them happen, usually pretty quickly. Sometimes that
is exactly what my surroundings need to get them unstuck.
But I'm not sure if a succession process goes very well when
the potential successor is an activator. I flared my nostrils too
many times. Sometimes I was too eager to be the next senior
pastor and not eager enough to be the associate pastor.

There were times when my desire to possess that title
(senior pastor) was silently killing off the gentle breeze of
my real self, which doesn't have a title. But it was so alluring.

Terry, the executive director (and my good friend), said
that working with me was sometimes like sitting in traffic
when nothing is moving and everybody is frustrated, but
some guy keeps honking his horn anyway. Another time he
told me that I kept veering into other people's lanes, merg-
ing into their areas of responsibility. He was right on both
counts. Another time he mentioned how difficult leading
this church was because the engine needed to be replaced
even though we couldn't stop the car.

Terry really likes car metaphors.

After about four years, Dave and I were preaching roughly
the same number of weekends per year. I saw this as the natu-
ral progression toward me becoming the next senior pastor.
Then one day, during a board meeting, the board members
said they wanted Dave to significantly increase his preaching
load. This came out of the blue (at least for me), and I balked.

"But that means I'll be preaching a lot less," I blurted.

I felt as though something that had been given to me had been ripped from my hands. I did the math in my head. Instead of preaching twenty or so times a year, I'd be preaching twelve or thirteen times. I loved preaching. It was hard to swallow a reality in which I'd preach less.

As time went on, my dream continued to dissipate, and my mood grew dark. I kept telling myself to have patience, to do my actual job instead of working so hard to earn a job that hadn't been offered to me yet. Sometimes that worked.

At one point, some members of the board gently questioned my compatibility. One of them suggested that I was built for speed, like a Ferrari, and that the church was built more like a Clydesdale, plodding along slowly but surely toward a destination at which they would arrive someday. I hated that comparison, even though it did hold some truth. I interpreted it as a lack of confidence in me, and perhaps it was. But it was also the result of someone simply trying to figure out why things kept going so sideways.

We agreed that we needed a time of mutual discernment to see if we should keep pursuing the idea of succession. The board put me through a life-coaching process with an outside firm that has a unique and very thorough process of listening to stories of a person's life to determine the things he or she is best at and is motivated to accomplish.

What I found out was encouraging but not all that surprising. I was wired to be a leader in an organization in which I could empower people to discover latent gifts they didn't know they had. They said I'd be happiest if I could *create* culture through my leadership and preaching.

The culture of this church was very embedded and unique. It was not a place where I would be able to *create* culture.

"You keep crossing into other people's lanes and honking your horn in traffic," they told me, "because you aren't doing what you are wired by God to do: You are most happy and most fulfilled when you're creating environments in which people's latent gifts can emerge. For whatever reason, you aren't doing that there."

It was liberating to hear, but it was also very painful. I'll never forget a conversation I had with a mentor of mine while sitting by a large, ancient tree. I told him what was happening to my dream of being the senior pastor at this church.

"Perhaps it's time to let it go," he said with sadness in his voice.

Where are you going?

This is an exciting question when you suspect you know the answer. For years, I had imagined myself in the role of senior pastor at this church. It felt right. It felt comfortable. It felt scary, but I felt up to the challenge.

But when the bottom falls out of your dream, *Where are you going?* begins to feel like a desperate question. Mary and I had dozens of long conversations about what this all meant. She loved this church, too, and at first she really didn't want to leave. Neither did I. Letting go of the dream that would have secured a very public success was extremely difficult. Becoming senior pastor would have felt like *validation*.

Approval and Admiration were cheering me on to get this job, no matter what.

But staying would have betrayed a very private secret: The way I see to the shalom of my brothers and sisters is to *create* environments in which people's latent gifts can emerge.

When you get close to discovering what your secret is— how you see to the shalom of your brothers and sisters— there will almost always be a tempting alternative that is close but not quite it. It's a wise person who waits for the real thing and resists that which seems "close enough."

———•———

Abram's story is perhaps the strangest in all the beguiling stories in the Scriptures. We know nothing of Abram's childhood, which is odd considering we're told so much of the rest of the patriarchs' childhoods. We know that Abram is from the land of Ur, that his father is Terah, and that he is childless. At first we have no record of his faith or his righteousness. He is not special in any obvious way. He's stuck in Haran, where his father has taken the family.

Bruce Feiler, one of my favorite writers on the history of the Hebrew Scriptures, wrote, "Our chief reaction upon meeting him is not admiration; it's indifference or pity. He's the ultimate blank slate: childless and childhood-less."[1]

Abram is not successful in any discernable way. He's the antihero. He's a nobody. If this were a movie, we'd be unimpressed with the main character. We'd turn it off.

Abram knows almost nothing—maybe nothing at all—about the God who calls to him. While Moses will later be told many things about God when he receives his calling at the burning bush, Abram gets only a few words.

Go from your country and your kindred and your
father's house to the land that I will show you. I will
make of you a great nation, and I will bless you,
and make your name great, so that you will be a
blessing. I will bless those who bless you, and the one
who curses you I will curse; and in you all the families
of the earth shall be blessed.   GENESIS 12:1-3

God seems to have been searching for an ordinary human being, without credentials, to begin a new creation of a people who would see to the shalom of the world; a community that would love God and represent what God is like to the rest of the world.

Abram didn't really know anything about God, but he went anyway, not even knowing where he was going. Perhaps he went because his long-held dream of having children seemed to be about to come true: "I will make of you a great nation," God had said. So he went.

But even after he went, he remained childless. Sometimes your dream ends up shattered on the floor, even when it seemed as though God promised that it would happen. It's one thing to read the story and glean insights. It's another thing to live out the story in real time. Can you imagine having to wait all that time? Can you imagine what would happen to your faith? *Did God really say that I would become a great nation? Did I just imagine this whole thing?*

Feiler wrote,

> In a story about creation, he cannot create. He is the anti-God.
>
> Which may be the point . . .
>
> The lesson of Abraham's early life is that being human is not being safe, or comfortable. Being human is being uncertain, being on the way to an unknown place. Being on the way to God. The emptiness of Abraham's invisible youth is the triumph of recognizing this necessity. His early years are a questioning, a yearning, a growing desperation, and finally a humble plea.[2]

Can you remember a time when you were uncertain, on your way to an unknown place? How did you feel? What words would you use to characterize that time? Maybe you're there now. Maybe your questioning has turned into a yearning, a growing desperation, and finally a humble plea. What is your honest question for God right now?

God eventually changed Abram's name to Abraham, meaning he would become "the father of many nations" (Genesis 17:4, MSG). "Abraham was chosen not for his sake," Feiler wrote, "but for the sake of the world."

Abram's unlikely story makes me wonder if we miss

opportunities for restoration because of our need for certainty and our inability to live with our questioning, our yearning, and our growing desperation.

I wonder if we never get to where we need to go because we're unwilling to simply be "on the way to God." I wanted to know exactly when I was going to be senior pastor and why it wasn't happening, and I demanded a lot of answers.

Lech lecha is the Hebrew phrase that is translated as "go" in Genesis 12:31. *Lech* means "go." When you add *lecha* to the end of it, it's personalizing the command. *Lecha* means "for you" or "to you."

Lech lecha is like God saying to Abram, "Hey! I'm talking to *you*! Get yourself going!"

Rashi (the great medieval commentator) understood *lech lecha* literally. He translated it as "go for you." Rashi wrote that the command means "Go for your own enjoyment and for your own good." He understood the command as an invitation to adventure and self-discovery.[3]

Do you have the courage to wait to see the place God will show you? Even in your desperation, can you believe that you're being led to a place of wonder and self-discovery, for your own enjoyment and for your own good?

When I decided to leave the church that I loved, I knew I was still a pastor. I knew I wanted to lead and preach. I wanted to create the kind of culture in which people's latent God-given gifts could emerge and flourish. And that is when the idea of planting a church slowly began to emerge, like a blazing and beautiful sunrise after a long, dark night.

After dozens of conversations with Mary and close friends, after countless prayers of desperation and some excitement, I told Dave and the board that I needed to leave to plant a church. I was forty-three years old. They were gracious and also quite surprised. Though they affirmed my sense of motivation and calling, it brought up lots of questions for them and some pain. It happened a lot quicker than they had thought it would. At the end of it all, they blessed Mary and me, prayed for us, and sent us out.

In May 2014, I started having conversations with people about starting a church called Genesis. Our stated vision was to join God's work of "cultivating new beginnings in all of us, everywhere." Those first few months were exhilarating, exhausting, and sometimes frightening. As I stared at spreadsheets with projected expenses of staff and equipment, I became an expert at asking people to give—financially and with their time, gifts, and passions. We dreamed of starting something that felt warm, small, and ancient but progressive. We wouldn't use screens to project words; we'd use liturgy bulletins that people could hold and bring home, with beautiful prayers written out, which we would recite together. We'd be guided by the seasons of the church calendar. We'd follow the lectionary—a three-year cycle of Scripture readings that would keep us anchored in the story of God. We'd partner with organizations that are meeting the needs of vulnerable children and those who are exploited in the world.

Mary and I spent a long weekend at my parents' cabin, writing and talking and dreaming. Our church's guiding values emerged slowly out of that time, and I love them:

- *Simplicity.* We want to stay responsive to what's important, so we order our lives and our community in ways that leave margin and space, where we live within our limits. We are intentional and wise in our choices and our commitments.

- *Conversation.* We ask lots of questions that show interest in people and in process. We're better when we're talking and learning, so we allow great questions to lead us together toward what's good and true. We can be confident in sharing and hearing ideas, because we know God is more and better than anything we can name.

- *Rhythms.* We honor the Sabbath, we follow the lectionary, and we're learning spiritual practices. We are countercultural in how we create space to hear from God in our lives and in our worship gatherings. We follow the seasons of the church calendar—finding daily, weekly, and yearly rhythms that help us stay rooted in the story of God.

- *Attentiveness.* We believe that God is actively at work at all times and places, making all things new. Because we want to join that work, we spend time praying for and seeking a restored way of seeing, hearing, and sensing God, one another, and our own souls.

- *Restoration.* What is made new in us is there to join in the work of making *all things new*. A part of this work is to be aware of and present to suffering people in a broken world, as well as using our gifts to alleviate that suffering. God breathes life into us so that we can be a healing presence in the world.

- *Ordinariness.* Most of us live our lives *as if* we need to be more and different and better in order to be significant. We want to live our lives *as is*—embracing who we are and where we are, believing that our gifts, our lives, our vocations—as small or large as they might be—are where God will be present to us and active through us. We believe that we can bless others by being *who* we actually are and operating from *where* we actually are.

- *Delight.* We try to respond to what is beautiful and good with wonder, celebration, joy, gratitude, and love. We also try to smile, laugh, and enjoy one another. What delights us leads us into doing all kinds of good in the world.

That was two years ago. We are now a growing, intergenerational family of people who are seeing new beginnings in ourselves and others.

There is Carol, my favorite seventy-three-year-old, who sits in a wheelchair, a blanket covering her even in the summertime. She buried three husbands, has multiple sclerosis, just had painful hip surgery, and keeps talking about her own new beginnings.

And there is Pam, who is approaching her sixties and can't stop dreaming. She and her husband, Will, were quite wealthy, with kids and big toys and lots of traveling, before they were ambushed by God's love and a new vision for their family. Then they lost most of their money and had to start over. Pam wants to create places of healing for people who are hurting and broken.

And there is Trynica, the ten-year-old who decided to run a 5K on her birthday to raise more than $1,000 for women caught in sex trafficking. Trynie (as we call her) is hopeful, delightful, responsible, and a gifted speaker. We've had her share poems at church, something she takes very seriously. Genesis is a place from which she is rising and becoming powerful.

And there is me.

Church planting can be a treacherous place for someone addicted to approval and admiration. I'm learning to take myself less seriously when attendance numbers drop. I'm learning to resolve conflict and stay engaged in a long obedience in the same direction rather than chasing the next exciting thing.[4] I'm learning to explore my joy and also touch my limits.

I'm learning that I really can't be a successful pastor.

But I am learning that I can be a *restored* pastor. Restoring what's broken isn't just about crawling on your hands and knees through glass until you're bloody and broken. *Lech lecha*, following the understanding of Rashi, means that my

own joy and enjoyment *matter* in measuring at least some
of the metrics for indicating a successful Steve. I think I'm
starting to learn that I can be a joyful pastor. Not a driven
one, not a busy one, not a heroic one.

I didn't know any of that was in store for me when I let
go of the dream of being the next senior pastor at that big,
beautiful church. How could I have known?

I hadn't gone where I needed to go yet.

———•———

Where are *you* being called to go, where you're not certain
of the outcome?

When Abram left his family to go to a place God would
show him, he showed us that we often walk a painful and
sometimes confusing journey. He taught us that we can leave
the familiar for the unfamiliar, no matter what it is. Even
the most familiar thing about Abram—his very name—was
changed (see Genesis 17:5). My friend Alan, who is a rabbi,
says that adding the letter *h* to Abram's name is essentially
expanding Abram to hold God in his *very identity* (the letter
h is used twice in the name of God—YHWH).

When you get quiet with God, and with others, are you
being sent somewhere?

Does it have to do with raising your child with disabilities?

Does it have to do with healing after a painful divorce?

Does it have to do with reconciling a relationship that
feels broken beyond repair?

Does it have to do with moving somewhere you don't want to go?

Does it have to do with exploring silence and solitude?

Does it involve pursuing the dream that involves risk and potential failure and loss of security?

Does it mean learning to live with chronic pain?

Does it mean widening your circle to love someone with whom you disagree?

Does it mean working less and listening more?

Does it mean going to counseling?

What do you need to embrace and what do you need to walk away from so that you can *lech lecha*? Seeking wholeness is always about leaving one place and going somewhere else. It requires movement. It's almost always painful, and very often you don't really know where you're going until long after you leave.

> *May you have the courage to leave the familiar*
> *place behind so that you can go to the place that*
> *God will show you, and may you be enlarged so that*
> *you can hold God in your very identity as you go.*

QUESTIONS *for Reflection & Discussion*

1. The chapter started with a quote from *The Fellowship of the Ring*, a wise piece of advice that Bilbo gives to Frodo: "It's a dangerous business, Frodo, going out of your door. . . . You

step into the Road, and if you don't keep your feet, there is no knowing where you might be swept off to." What part of this quote resonates with your own experience of "going out of your door"? What do you think Bilbo means by "keep[ing] your feet?"

2. Steve wrote about how he dealt with letting go of a long-held dream to be a senior pastor at a particular church. What dreams have you had to let go of, and how has that affected you?

3. Can you think of a time when you felt as if you were called by God to "go to a place that God would show you"? Where did you go, and how did you get there? What did you have to leave in order to go?

4. Going to a place that God will show you requires the ability to hear God's voice, which can be a very tricky thing. How do you personally try to determine if it's God's voice, your own voice, or some combination of the two?

5. Where does it seem as though you are being called to "go" these days? What excites you about that call? What scares you? What do you need in order to "go out of your door"?

WHAT WILL YOU BRING?

*Learn what it means to experience something fully, then drop it and move
on to the next moment, uninfluenced by the previous one. You'd be traveling
with such little baggage that you could pass through the eye of a needle.*

ANTHONY DE MELLO, *Awareness*

IT'S POSSIBLE to go somewhere else without going anywhere
different.

I was in New York City recently, and one of my friends
had forgotten shampoo. So we went to Target, like you do
when you're in New York City. And even in New York, Target
is laid out exactly as all the rest of them are. And the moment
we got inside, my friend said, "Ahh, this feels like home."
Why else is every Target laid out the same, no matter which
city you find yourself in?

Why else is there a McDonald's in Moscow?

Why else do you think it's a good idea to stay in that
mind-numbing job?

One reason we seek out McRibs in Russia and Target in Times Square is because we want to feel equipped for the task. To go to a new place is to leave behind an old place and all that is attached to it, all that is known about it. We actually need to be liberated from the old place to keep ourselves from bringing it along with us to the new place.

Just because you knew how to do your last job or raise your previous child or relate to that previous person, it doesn't mean you'll have any clue about how to perform well in that new job or raise the next child or know what that new person likes and does not like.

If you're seeking wholeness, you're *always* being led to go somewhere, and you will *always* need to rediscover what to bring with you and what to leave behind.

Every time you start a new job.

Every time you have a child.

Every time you enter a new relationship.

Every time you attempt a DIY project at home.

Every time you give the car keys to your teenage children.

Every time you follow a wild idea.

Every time you try to quit something you've tried to quit before.

If you know exactly what to bring with you, you're most likely *not* going to the place that God will show you. You're simply going to a place you've already been, even if you've never been there. You're not seeking wholeness if you insist on bringing what you've always brought and doing what you've always done in every new situation in which you find yourself.

The journey of restoration requires things that you can acquire only after you've left home.

The problem is that when you get closer and closer to naming your secret—the way in which you will see to the shalom of your brothers and sisters—you might assume you know what to bring with you.

Most likely, you do not.

—•—

I grew up in Oxnard, California, but I never learned how to surf. Ever since I moved away in 1983, it's been a dream of mine to learn. So when I found myself in Laguna Beach last year to spend time with some good friends and do some writing, I decided to take surfing lessons with my friend Charlie. Charlie came into my life at a very low moment five years ago, and he's been a steady companion since then.

After paying fifty dollars and signing up for the surfing lessons, I got an e-mail explaining how things would work. We were supposed to meet just south of Thalia Street Beach. The surfing school would provide the wet suits and surfboards. We were told to bring towels, sunscreen, water, *etc.*

What is the *etc?*

I have come to believe that *etc*, in any sense, really means those extra things you're going to need that I can't even begin to tell you about, because it has to do with what's really essential for *you*; it's specific to what *you'll* need, and only *you* can discover what that is.

It's a wise person who discovers what his or her *etc* is and then has the courage to carry it on the journey toward restoration. More on that later . . .

I was excited to become a surfer. I had two huge blue towels under my arm—one for me and one for Charlie—as I walked down the steep hill toward the ocean. I passed a man with a long, thin ponytail who was wearing dark blue jeans and accompanied by a tiny dog. I walked past a teenage couple saying good-bye to each other, or maybe it was hello—I wasn't sure. If their hands gave any clues, they seemed to really, really like each other. I walked past Orange Inn, a great local breakfast spot where I had eaten twice, despite its dubious claims[1] of being home to the original smoothie and having the best coffee in town.

Heading south a block or two from Orange Inn, I turned right on Thalia and walked about fifty steps down to the beach. As my toes dug into the sand, I smelled seaweed and saltwater, the body odor of the Pacific Ocean. I love that smell. It takes me all the way back to my childhood.

When the lesson began, we were told to pick out a used wet suit and put it on (imagine trying to put on really tight, wet, rubber skinny jeans two sizes too small, but for your whole body). After I squeezed into mine, we were told to pick a surfboard. There were about ten of them, of various sizes, lying on the sand.

The smaller ones looked cooler; the larger ones looked like king-size beds. The instructor told us that the bigger the board, the easier it was. There were two or three huge blue planks, which they called aircraft carriers. There was no way I was picking one of those. Even though I was anticipating it would be more difficult to get up on the smaller board, some prehistoric part of me needed to look cool and more experienced than I actually was, so I picked a smaller board.

I think maybe you see where this is going.

Next we had a short lesson onshore about paddling past the break. We practiced "popping up" in one fluid motion, going from lying on our stomachs to perching on our boards with our knees bent. (Note: This is not even really all that easy on the sand when your board is not moving at all—just saying.) Following a few lame attempts, I was slightly winded and not very confident. Then we headed out into the water.

After we had paddled out past the break, I looked around and saw a few people sitting on their boards in the water, nonchalantly chatting and laughing. I thought they looked pretty cool. So I flipped my legs in the water and tried sitting on my board.

Let me be very clear about this important point: I'd much rather be immediately awesome at something than have to learn it. Maybe you're thinking that's a universal feeling, but I promise you I feel it more acutely than most.

The awful truth is that I was having major problems merely *sitting* on my board. I kept trying to find the spot where I wouldn't wobble and then slide into the ocean. I slid forward so that the nose was underwater. That didn't work. I slid way back so the nose was a foot or two out of the water. That didn't work either. I kept trying to talk to a few other newbies, kept trying to laugh and be chill, but I just kept sliding off that board into the water while they were trying to say something to me.

Things got even worse when I attempted to catch an actual wave and "pop up" on the board. After trying once on the small board and failing utterly, I traded with someone else for one of the aircraft carriers. I did a little better on that, but I only made it up on one wobbly knee before falling back into the surf. I tried a few more times, but I never did stand up.

I was ready to get out of the water when I saw Charlie on the shore (he was in the group behind mine). Seeing my last attempt, he laughed and waved, as if trying to say, "That was really bad, but I like you!"

It was a few hours after those surfing lessons when I realized that for the whole time, I wasn't learning how to surf. I was only trying really hard not to look stupid. I was focusing on how defective I felt because I wasn't automatically great at this really hard sport. I was feeling like a loser because I couldn't even *sit* on the board, much less *ride* it (which *is* pretty lame, even objectively).

I realized that because I was trying so hard to get it right, I was completely missing out on surfing. I was defining *surfing* as "exceling at surfing" and not simply "learning to surf." I was so afraid of getting it wrong that it was impossible to get it right in any real sense that mattered.

Have you ever done something that seemed insignificant at the time, but it proved to be a turning point? Have you ever been lucky enough to realize it?

There was an invitation for me in that ocean, and it was all about what I was going to bring with me for this next leg of the journey, the one where I'd plant a church and begin to write books.

It was about what I needed to bring with me and what I needed to leave behind.

It was an invitation to discover what my *etc* was: those extra things I was going to need that other people couldn't even begin to tell me about because they had to do with what's really essential for *me*—specific to what *I* needed— and only *I* could discover what they were.

While failing at being a surfer in the ocean that day, I realized I no longer wanted to bring Approval and Admiration with me wherever it was that I was going. I realized how much fun had been choked out of my life because of my need to get things right the first time versus learning how to do them like everybody else. It had harmed my marriage and my parenting. It had affected my ability to be a pastor. It had kept me from admitting I was a human being with needs and limits and imperfections.

I realized I was going to need to learn how to be okay with being a learner. I'm aware how shallow this sounds, but honestly, for most of my life, I've been trying so hard to impress people (even the people who love me for me, such as my wife and my closest friends). This is an exhausting way to live.

Your own *etc* is personal and unique. Sometimes it's certain people who come at just the right time. Sometimes it's a specific learning gleaned from failure. Sometimes it's a whisper from God right when you need it. Sometimes it's remembering what you really love. For me, in the Pacific Ocean, my *etc* involved beginning to learn to be present—and even grateful—for the radical incompleteness of not knowing how to do something.

———•———

When Jesus sent out his disciples, he was kind enough to pair them up two by two. He gave them authority to deal with evil opposition, for which I suppose they may have gulped, eyes wide with fear. But what he didn't give them was equally disturbing:

> He ordered them to take nothing for their journey
> except a staff; no bread, no bag, no money in their
> belts; but to wear sandals and not to put on two
> tunics. He said to them, "Wherever you enter a house,
> stay there until you leave the place. If any place will
> not welcome you and they refuse to hear you, as
> you leave, shake off the dust that is on your feet as a
> testimony against them." MARK 6:8-11

It seems as though Jesus was stacking the deck against them. No money? No food? No extra tunic? Really? This seems like some sort of bizarre hazing ritual.

Or perhaps it was a brilliant way to teach them how to leave behind what they'd known so they would have to meet new people and experience new things on their own terms. I think Jesus was teaching them how to enter new places without relying on their usual bag of tricks, or their charm, or anything other than the stark reality of possibility.

He was teaching them what to bring and what not to bring, but he couldn't teach them all the same thing because each one of them needed to discover what his own unique *etc* was. And he would only discover it by leaving home with as little as possible.

Sometimes the only way to find your *etc* is by getting it wrong, getting lost, or falling off your surfboard in front of a bunch of people who are getting it right.

My friend Keith calls this kind of knowing "experiential knowledge." There is a certain kind of wisdom that is only gained by finding out what you *don't know*.

I trust people who know what they *don't know*.

You know?

And just like I felt stupid in the ocean that day in Laguna Beach as I kept sliding off my surfboard, I wonder if those disciples stumbled more than a few times. They most likely got it wrong more than they got it right.

But I also wonder if, at some point, they experienced the wide-open freedom of releasing the need to know and the need to control their environment. Because they brought nothing other than one another and the power that Jesus anointed them with, they saw and experienced a level of transformation you don't get to experience if you insist on bringing your expertise.

You may be in a situation right now that's brand new, and you have no idea what you have with you that will work, and you feel utterly incompetent. Unprepared. Destined for failure. Afraid.

You need to know something else. Before Jesus sends you anywhere, he asks you to come and *be with him*, because he *wants you*.

> He went up the mountain and *called to him those whom he wanted*, and they came to him. And he appointed twelve, whom he also named apostles, *to be with him*, and to be sent out to proclaim the message, and to have authority to cast out demons.
>
> MARK 3:13-15, EMPHASIS ADDED

Have you ever experienced the thrill of being wanted and invited into something special? It's so much better than being good at something. It's so much better than being admired or being successful. It's also so much more vulnerable and risky.

A few years ago, my son Elijah got a bad rash all over his body, so I took him to urgent care. We read books in the waiting room. We talked. I helped him pick out a sticker on the way out. A few days later, he asked me if we could *go back* to the doctor's office.

I smiled. "Why do you want to go back to the doctor's office?" I asked him.

"I liked being with just you, Dad—just you and me," he said.

Do you believe it's possible that Jesus calls you to be with him primarily because he wants you and wants to be with you?

I've been a pastor for more than twenty years, and my experience is that most people believe that they're an agenda for Jesus. They believe Jesus just wants to change them, clean them up, and send them out. He's available for triage when they mess up, but he's mostly miffed because there's a whole world out there that needs saving, and our own petty troubles and anxieties are wasting his time.

I am more convinced than ever that what restores us most fully is the belief that Jesus wants us to be with him, exactly as we are and not as we should be, and that he is not in a hurry for us to change right away.

It's God's kindness that leads to repentance (see Romans 2:4). *Repentance* simply means changing your mind about where you're going in order to be made whole. Our wholeness—our restoration—is a result of God's kindness, not God's determination that we get it right.

Jesus took these disciples into his life and opened up his humanity to them. He taught them, laughed with them, ate with them, and stayed up late into the night talking to them. He encouraged them. He challenged them. I can imagine each of them opening up like flowers in the springtime.

Determining your own *etc*—those extra things you're going to need that I can't even begin to tell you about because it has to do with what's really essential for *you*; it's specific to what *you'll* need, and only *you* can discover what that is—is not something you can study for and then pass, like a test.

You'll only find out your *etc* by leaving what is familiar and taking only that which you discover you need while you're on the way there. Fortunately, we're not sent out alone on that journey. And, thank goodness, we are called to be with Jesus before we are even sent out.

——•——

On that same trip to Laguna Beach, Charlie and I went to a Pete Holmes show. Pete Holmes is a hilarious comedian who mixes raw honesty with real hope. He told a story about a time when he got drunk and ate a chicken quesadilla, even though he's a vegan. He described the shame loop that was on repeat in his mind—about what a stupid mistake he had made, what a stupid person he was.

Then he paused and did a quintessential Pete Holmes thing, which is to make you belly laugh one moment and cry the next. He said, "Whenever I catch myself doing that, I simply repeat, as many times as it takes, 'I love you, Peter.'"[2]

And then he admitted how good that chicken quesadilla tasted.

There are four words I'll never hear from Approval and Admiration: "I love you, Steve."

As you travel your own road toward wholeness,
may you come to know that you need only bring
your dependence and your trust in the one who
calls you to be with him, not because you're an
agenda but because he wants *to be with you.*

QUESTIONS *for Reflection & Discussion*

1. In what areas of your life are you choosing to stay with what you know—such as going to a McDonald's in Moscow—even though you feel prompted to take a new path?

2. Steve wrote about trying to learn how to surf and how he came to realize he was failing at life because he felt the need to succeed at everything right away. How does this resonate with you?

3. What do you think your *etc* is (those extra things you're going to need that other people can't even begin to tell you about because it has to do with what's really essential for *you*; it's specific to what *you'll* need, and only *you* can discover what that is)?

4. What are some things you think you might need to let go of so that you can go on the journey God is calling you toward?

5. In Mark 3:13-15, we read that Jesus called those disciples *he wanted, that they might be with him.* When you think about being called on a journey because Jesus wants you before you *do* anything—that you might be with him—how does that change how you think about the journey?

6

THE EXODUS

You come to God not by being strong, but by being weak;
not by being right, but through your mistakes.

RICHARD ROHR

THE HEBREW LANGUAGE is best understood as describing a people *in action*, moving from here to there. Genesis is all about movement: out of the Garden, out of Haran, out of Canaan, and finally into Egypt.

Many scholars see Genesis (which means "beginning") as the prequel to the real story of the Hebrew people, which starts in Exodus. Exodus opens by describing a people who are *not moving at all*. They're stuck as slaves in Egypt; they're not going anywhere, and they haven't been going anywhere for hundreds of years. They spend their days making bricks to build monuments for gods they don't know or believe in. Over and over again, they groan in their slavery and cry out to God for deliverance and relief (see Exodus 2:23).

The Hebrew language uses a rigid economy of words to convey a kaleidoscope of meaning and destiny, transcending time, looping backward and forward, sewing us all together in a fabric of shared story. If you want to understand how Hebrew words are used in the Scriptures, you need to know that they are all based on a parent root word, which then has children and adopted children.

Root words do a lot of heavy lifting. They flex and expand; they morph and adapt to describe many different sides of reality. In Hebrew, a root is a word (usually three letters)—without vowels or inflection—that conveys a meaning. It is not a verb or a noun per se. In English, the differences between nouns and verbs are straightforward: A noun expresses a person, place, or thing, while a verb expresses action. In Hebrew, it's less straightforward: A verb is a word for the *action* of a person, place, or thing; and a noun is a word for a person, place, or thing *in action*.

Let's take the noun *matsor*, which is built from a root (*mtsr*). The root carries a meaning such as "hindering" or "restraining." It then is inflected to express the noun *matsor*, which could be something like "a siege" or "an affliction." It could also be inflected to express a verb with a meaning such as "to restrain."

Matsor keeps people stuck where they don't want to be.

Matsor can describe anything that traps you and limits your freedom. It's anything that attempts to restrain or hinder you.

Matsor may be the drive you feel to achieve more in order to be significant.

Matsor may be the relationship in which you feel marginalized and dehumanized.

Matsor may be the alcohol you consume to numb your anger or alleviate your boredom.

Matsor may be the Internet, which keeps you up late into the night in search of relief from the stress of your job or your kids.

Matsor may be the religious dogma you stubbornly cling to, even though it's driving you away from every relationship that matters to you.

Matsor may be the country in which you live.

Matsor may be the smartphone that you grab anytime there's even one second of downtime.

Matsor may be the job that demands more hours from you than is healthy to give.

Matsor may be the flickering images of pornography that disgust you but from which you can't seem to escape.

Matsor enslaves you and then tricks you into believing you need the shackles to survive.

Egypt is of course a physical place with a people and a history, but it can also describe a state of being. The word for "Egypt" in Hebrew is *Mitsrayim*, a child word from the same root word as *matsor*. *Mitsrayim* means "narrow." *Mitsrayim* represents anything that enslaves you or fragments you, trapping you in a narrow place. Egypt is narrow topographically, but it also represents the experience of being in a narrow place spiritually.

Ever been there?

"Oh no," Dee said, sitting across the table from me at Breaking Bread Café in North Minneapolis.

"What?" I asked cautiously. I had been talking to her about the Exodus as a broad theological concept that I was interested in writing and preaching about.

"I always get nervous when white pastors use the Exodus narrative and act as though they're the children of Israel instead of the Egyptians."

Sometimes your sister sees to your shalom by helping you see something that you didn't see.

Dee and I are both church planters in our denomination who are learning what it means to see to the shalom of Minneapolis. Dee is one of the best preachers I've ever heard. She's prophetic, wise, funny, and passionate, and she's more than six feet tall. She's a powerful presence, and she's becoming a good friend.

And Dee is black.

When Dee spoke at our church three weeks after a police officer shot and killed Jamar Clark, a twenty-four-year-old black man who lived in North Minneapolis, she invited our mostly white church to lament. She preached about Hanani, whom we learn about in the biblical account of Nehemiah. Hanani—Nehemiah's brother—came to him and told him how it really was with the children of Israel and with the city of Jerusalem itself.

It takes great courage for someone to inhabit a place that has been destroyed and then to go back and tell others, who weren't there, how things really are. Sometimes people who haven't been there don't want to hear about it. Sometimes they work very hard to keep you quiet.

Hanani said, "The exile survivors who are left there in the province are in bad shape. Conditions are appalling. The wall of Jerusalem is still rubble; the city gates are still cinders" (Nehemiah 1:3, MSG).

When Nehemiah heard Hanani's report, he sat down and wept. He mourned for days. He fasted and prayed to God.

Dee lives in North Minneapolis, where the shooting occurred. And when she sat on a small wooden stool on the large stage at our church that day, she told us that she was Hanani, coming from North Minneapolis to tell us how it was with the people of North Minneapolis and the city itself.

She told us about the prayers and the singing. She told us about hope rising. She also told us about the fear and the rage that her neighbors were feeling. She asked us to lament, to grieve. She asked us to mourn and fast and pray. She asked us to see and hear what was happening.

She gave us a great gift, though an uncomfortable and risky one. She helped us understand the *matsor* that our black brothers and sisters in North Minneapolis feel every day.

I know it's uncomfortable to read the Exodus story and consider the possibility that you're an Egyptian. Stay with me. We can't talk about restoring the entire world if we don't talk about repenting of our part in breaking it.

Sometimes, seeing to the shalom of your brothers and sisters puts you in a position in which you need to realize you have been part of the *matsor* that has kept them enslaved, even if you haven't knowingly done anything to keep them enslaved.

And Moses is a perfect candidate to lead us there.

Moses was a person with an identity crisis. Though he was Hebrew by nature, he was raised in an Egyptian household, with Egyptian values, from infancy until well into his adulthood. It's why he thought he could see to the shalom of his brothers and sisters by murdering the Egyptian slave driver.

When we don't really know the life of someone who is enslaved, we tend to resort to answers that don't really help.

It took Moses forty years in the wilderness to take Egypt out of him.

If Egypt was in Moses, it's possible that it's also in me.

Let's stop for a second. If you're white like me and you're being asked to put yourself in the position of the Egyptians in the Exodus narrative, what feelings rise up in you?

Maybe you're tired of hearing about white privilege.

Maybe you see riots happening and are sickened by the violence that the media captures.

Maybe you feel guilty.

Maybe you feel defensive. You're not a racist.

Maybe you want to go do something, now, to fix it, because you see that it isn't right.

Maybe you're afraid when you think of building relationships with people of color who might be angry with you because you are white.

Maybe you think it isn't your battle because it isn't happening in your neighborhood.

I've had every one of those feelings, and I still do.

And yet, Dee is my sister. I'm her brother. By opening up to me and telling me that she gets nervous when white folks like me use the Exodus narrative as if they're the children of Israel, she's seeing to my shalom. Restoring what's broken in me, you, and the entire world means that we have to change our definition of who our family is.

It gets especially interesting—and transformative—when we *enter* the Scriptures rather than just *read* them.

You're *reading* the story of Moses when you cheer for Moses and wonder why Pharaoh was so hard-hearted and didn't just let those people go.

But you've *entered* the story of Moses when you realize that you're afraid to go where God leads you and you ask God to send someone else.

You're reading the story of the children of Israel when you skip quickly over the fact that four hundred years is nearly twice as long as the United States of America has existed.

But you've entered the story of the children of Israel when you cry out in your own slavery and hear nothing from God except silence for years and years.

I'm reading the story of Pharaoh when I wonder why he doesn't just let God's people go, especially after all those gruesome plagues.

But I've entered the story when I realize that I'm also Pharaoh. I sometimes resist God's voice and God's desire to restore the entire world. I sometimes act as if God only wants to restore *me*.

"Let my people go," God sometimes says to me.
How will I answer?
Where will my answer take me?
What will I need to bring with me on *that* journey?

————————

There's another notion at play in the Exodus narrative, and it changes everything. The Hebrew word *racham* can be a verb or a noun. When it's a verb, it expresses the *action* of a person, place, or thing. *Racham* is a word used to describe the action of someone who is showing deep affection, compassion, or mercy for someone else. It can also mean "to protect from harm." *Racham* is what you do when you show tender affection to someone else. One of my favorite places in the Hebrew Scriptures where this word is used is in Deuteronomy 30:3: "GOD, your God, will restore everything you lost; he'll have [*racham*] on you; he'll come back and pick up the pieces from all the places where you were scattered" (MSG).

When *racham* is a noun, it means "womb."

The God of your father—may he help you!
    And may The Strong God—may he give you his
        blessings,
Blessings tumbling out of the skies,
    blessings bursting up from the Earth—
    blessings of breasts and [*racham*].

GENESIS 49:25, MSG

Isn't it interesting that a womb—the place where a human being grows, is nourished, and is protected—comes from the same root meaning "tender affection, compassion, and mercy"? And isn't it interesting that a womb and a birth canal are very narrow (*matsor*) places, but they are necessary for new life to emerge?

To show compassion is essentially to provide a womb for someone, a place where he or she can be nourished and can grow in a safe place. Though the word *racham* isn't used in the Exodus narrative, God shows compassion, mercy, and deep affection for the children of Israel when he tells Moses what he is about to do:

> I have observed the misery of my people who are in
> Egypt; I have heard their cry on account of their task-
> masters. Indeed, I know their sufferings, and I have come
> down to deliver them from the Egyptians, and to bring
> them up out of that land to a good and broad land, a
> land flowing with milk and honey.   EXODUS 3:7-8

If we want to see to the shalom of those suffering under the withering captivity of *matsor* (whether it be the captive or the captor), we will need to bring with us the gentle breeze of *racham*, of compassion. And when we do, the rebirthing of many things becomes possible.

It's from compassion that the sacred future is created.

Compassion sits between two people who are different from each other and helps them understand each other.

Compassion doesn't try to fix things.

Compassion levels the playing field.

Compassion is the womb that allows reconciliation between enemies to grow and be nourished, even protected.

Compassion invites us to lament, grieve, and come alongside those who are enslaved and then to become participants in restoration rather than the managers of it.

Compassion is the prerequisite for genuine confession and repentance.

Compassion leads us to a whole new understanding of freedom.

——•——

On their way out of Egypt, the children of Israel found themselves once more in a narrow place, and they were terrified.

They were standing near the shore of the Red Sea, and they saw a huge cloud of dust rising miles in the distance, along with the glint of swords in the sun. They heard the sound of chariot wheels racing toward them. The soldiers weren't coming to kill them; they were coming to capture them and bring them back to Egypt.

They had left by way of the wilderness—a long line of grandmothers and uncles and babies and teenagers—and had just made camp "at Pi Hahiroth, between Migdol and the sea . . . on the shore of the sea opposite Baal Zephon" (Exodus 14:2, MSG).

Pi Hahiroth. Migdol. The sea. And Baal Zephon.

Let's take it slow.

One of the possible meanings of *Pi Hahiroth* is "mouth (Pi) of the cave, hole, or prison (Hahiroth)." This would carry special meaning in relation to the Exodus. When you're at the mouth of a prison, you're at both the entrance and exit. Remember, in Egypt in the time of Moses, there are no road signs announcing where you are. The writer is hinting at something potent.

When you've been enslaved for generations and then suddenly find yourself at the entrance of the prison, where are you?

Hiroth is closely related to the word *herut*, which means "freedom."

They aren't free yet, but the children of Israel can finally see the first shafts of light in more than four hundred years. So perhaps *Pi Hahiroth* can be translated as "the mouth of freedom." This "mouth of freedom" was located between Migdol and the sea.

Migdol means "tower," but it's also a fortified city on the Egyptian border, a high place upon which military watchmen could see for miles and miles. A place where a million sitting ducks could be plucked off one by one.

Baal Zephon means "the false god (Baal) of the hidden, or north (Zephon)." This is the god of the narrow place, the one that enslaves you and then tricks you into believing you need to be enslaved to survive (or that you need to enslave others to survive). Baal Zephon is staring down at them, mocking them, and attempting to draw them back to slavery.

The false god of the hidden doesn't stand there with a pitchfork in its hand, snarling and menacing. The false god of the hidden is deceptive. It's *crafty*. It looks like relief and sounds like entitlement.

It invites you to come home to the familiar bottle instead of the unfamiliar plodding of working your daily program. You deserve it.

It beckons you to agree with the mob mentality that silently oppresses minorities instead of disagreeing by peacefully protesting. Who are you to speak against the crowd?

It stares back at you from the mirror, shaming you for how you look, but then whispers that the only way to feel better is to fill yourself full of food.

You can be well *tomorrow*. The false god of the north persuades you to settle because, well, it could be worse.

And the sea is the sea. It may have been beautiful, but it was impassable. No boats were waiting for the children of Israel, and there were no bridges. They were trapped again and were terrified.

Don't just read this story; enter it. Can you remember a time when you were on the threshold of leaving something that had enslaved you for a long time? Maybe it was an abusive relationship or a terrible job or an addiction. Maybe it was a destructive way of thinking or unhealthy relational patterns or codependency.

Do you remember how, at the moment you were almost free, it hounded you and tried to trap you again? Do you remember how impossible crossing that "Red Sea" seemed?

Can you hear the taunts—from actual people but also from your mind—saying you'd never make it? Do you remember how terrified you were? What did you do in that moment of fear?

Why is it that your moment of potential freedom is usually associated with feelings of fear and danger? Is it because there's a part of you that wants to leave and a part that doesn't? It seems as though the journey of wholeness, like the Hebrew language itself, is always about movement. It's always about going someplace and leaving another place behind. That kind of movement is never easy. It can even bring out your worst.

In their fear, the children of Israel turned on Moses like a pack of wild dogs.

> As Pharaoh approached, the Israelites looked up and saw them—Egyptians! Coming at them!
>
> They were totally afraid. They cried out in terror to GOD. They told Moses, "Weren't the cemeteries large enough in Egypt so that you had to take us out here in the wilderness to die? What have you done to us, taking us out of Egypt? Back in Egypt didn't we tell you this would happen? Didn't we tell you, 'Leave us alone here in Egypt—we're better off as slaves in Egypt than as corpses in the wilderness.'"
>
> EXODUS 14:10-12, MSG

Now imagine being Moses. You're trying to lead a mob of terrified people out of a familiar slavery and into an unfamiliar freedom. If you thought you were the hero, you now realize that you're definitely not. *"Weren't the cemeteries large enough in Egypt so that you had to take us out here in the wilderness to die?"* That is some very creative complaining.

When you're afraid, you're sometimes tempted to go back to what you know instead of going forward to what you don't know. Even if what you know is not good for you. Even if you can remember feeling trapped in what you know.

Sometimes the slavery that is familiar seems better than the freedom that is unknown.

Have you ever met a dry drunk? That person is sober but still as angry and hurting as ever. He or she hasn't touched a drop for years but hasn't been able to experience freedom. Have you ever met judgmental Christians? They know the Scriptures backward and forward, but they haven't crossed through the mouth of freedom yet.

How do you know when you're standing at the mouth of freedom? How do you know you're about to leave the narrow place where you're trapped, hindered, and restrained?

You know you're standing at the mouth of freedom when you're terrified, when you're tempted to return to slavery, and when you've run out of your own resources.

If it doesn't look impossible, you're not at the mouth of freedom.

When you're trying to walk out of slavery and into freedom, and you're terrified, there's a radical trust you need to inhabit. You need to realize that you're not alone as you walk toward that water.

Moses spoke to the people: "Don't be afraid. Stand
firm and watch GOD do his work of salvation for you
today. Take a good look at the Egyptians today for
you're never going to see them again.

> GOD will fight the battle for you.
> And you? You keep your mouths shut!"

EXODUS 14:13-14, MSG

When I'm afraid, I want to fight or I want to run.
Standing still seems like the very worst thing to do. (I do
sometimes like telling people to keep their mouths shut—I'll
admit that.)

Fear is a prison that keeps you enslaved. It will shake
your bones and rattle your soul until you feel as if you
might get splintered apart in a million pieces. The invitation that Moses gives to the children of Israel on the day
they will eventually walk toward freedom is to simply not
run.

If you're trying to work for racial reconciliation and restoration, don't run. Don't abandon the work you've done.
Don't give up.

If you're trying to walk the path of sobriety, don't run.
Don't abandon your program. Don't give up.

If you're trying to forgive someone who has betrayed you,
don't run. Don't abandon your counseling or your process.
Don't give up.

If you're trying to go back to school to earn that degree

that everybody said you could never finish, don't run. You can do it.

If you're trying to walk out of any kind of Egypt, you need to know that at some point, you'll be tempted to run back to what's familiar, even if it's hurting you or hurting others. It's really hard work.

Freedom implies you have to start learning to trust in God and not in what is familiar. Freedom stands between frightened people and their enemies, and it shouts down the voice of Baal Zephon, false god of the hidden.

Maybe you've already run. Maybe you've run so many times you've lost count. You have no idea where you're going. Just be here right now, in this moment. Stand here and don't move. It's a wise person who doesn't demand more from the present than it can offer. And it's a wise person who learns that the present carries with it everything he or she needs.

Maybe it all comes down to a question: What do you want?

Thomas Merton wrote,

My Lord God, I have no idea where I am going.
I do not see the road ahead of me. I cannot know
for certain where it will end. Nor do I really know
myself, and the fact that I think I am following
your will does not mean that I am actually doing
so. But I believe that the desire to please you does
in fact please you. And I hope I have that desire
in all that I am doing. I hope that I will never do

anything apart from that desire. And I know that if I do this you will lead me by the right road, though I may know nothing about it. Therefore I will trust you always though I may seem to be lost and in the shadow of death. I will not fear, for you are ever with me, and you will never leave me to face my perils alone.[1]

You don't need to run, even if you're afraid, because God is ever with you, and God will never leave you to face your perils alone.

———•———

The children of Israel eventually made it through the Red Sea because God made a way through the impassable waters. There's obviously wide debate about how that really happened. A million people walking between two walls of water that hung there, suspended in midair? Huh?

But how does anyone leave any Egypt, if not by a miracle? Do we really believe there's a reasonable explanation that can be chalked up only to good decisions, willpower, and maybe a little bit of luck? Is that really a better explanation?

My friend Lisa was so depressed that she couldn't get out of her pajamas or take a shower. She used to love to cook and create things, but then the darkness got so dark that she didn't believe she'd ever see the sun again. I met her after she read my book *Beginnings*, which is all about how sometimes, something new can burst out of disaster. That's what she's experienced. She's back to cooking and creating, and she can't believe that it's true. A wall of water on both sides of a million people looks at least as challenging as what it took to set her free from her Egypt.

Martin Luther King Jr. let us in on his secret all those years ago, and his dream captivated a nation. A wall of water on both sides of a million people looks at least as challenging as seeing his dream realized. Yep, it'll take a miracle, and conversations such as the one I had with Dee are paving the way for it. We're learning that *compassion* is stronger than that which keeps you *stuck*. Compassion paves the way for miracles.

So I'm learning to ask a different question when I read the Bible: How do I need to *enter* this instead of just *reading* it? Egypt is a real place, but so is the mouth of freedom. Anytime I find myself up against the Red Sea, I know it'll take a miracle to get through it.

When you find yourself in Egypt, whether it's as Moses, the children of Israel, or even Pharaoh—and you know it—your next move is to cry out to God and watch as he does his work of salvation. And when you're invited to join God in that work, you need to find the courage to do it.

God hears those cries. God sees us when we're trapped, hindered, and restrained. God helps stuck people get unstuck.

That is very good news.

But once you have been led through the impassable waters of the Red Sea, you'll find yourself in a different place. You will be out of Egypt, but you won't be where you want to go—not yet.

To get to where you're going, you have to go through the wilderness. If Egypt was narrow, the wilderness is expansive. It stretches out forever. The wilderness is required curriculum for restoring what's broken in me, you, and the entire world.

If you want to learn to inhabit the Promised Land someday, there's no way around the wilderness.

May you have eyes to see where people are trapped in the narrow places of slavery of every kind. May you join with them as they cry out to God to be rescued. And may you walk with them into freedom.

QUESTIONS *for Reflection & Discussion*

1. What is your Egypt these days—the narrow place that hinders you, limits you, and restrains you?

2. Moses murdered an Egyptian because the Egyptian was mistreating his "brother." What are the injustices you see that make you angry? What is your response to your own anger? Do you push it down? Do you lash out? In what ways do you respond with more violence to the violence you see?

3. Have you ever been at the mouth of freedom, where you are full of fear but also full of hope that something finally might change? What happened? How did it change things?

4. What was your reaction to considering that there are ways you might be Egypt—or Pharaoh—in different situations in your life?

5. Are there any ways you are being called to go back to Egypt, your former narrow place, so that you can lead others out? If so, how are you feeling about going back? What are you afraid of? What helps you go back?

7

THE WILDERNESS

*I only went out for a walk, and finally concluded to stay out
till sundown, for going out, I found, was really going in.*

JOHN MUIR

HE WATCHED a single line of birds float along the horizon,
a wispy reminder of how far he was from home and how
he wasn't floating anywhere. He hadn't talked to anyone in
weeks. He hadn't eaten anything either, but his belly had
stopped rumbling. His eyes were slits that peered out of cav-
ernous sockets, following geckos as they darted in and out
of view. His mind had slowed with his breath, as if his body
were conserving something he would soon need.

He slowly fingered each rib, counting them, his own
bodily rosary. When he prayed, which was often, he felt that
flesh and the blood coursing beneath it. He thought about
the mystery of how his own body housed such potent blood.

He watched that blood trickle from his heel where he had scraped it on a sharp rock. He thought about flesh and blood in the wilderness, the place where dark plays with light, where the visible and the invisible aren't so separate at all.

It was the Friend who had led him there, of that he was certain, though he was less certain why he was led out into the wilderness. He looked down at his feet, mottled with the dust of this barren place, and he remembered the day in the river. It was on that day that the Friend had opened up his own soul, filling it with light and substance, a kind of heaviness that felt somehow both free and forever tethered to something. The Voice had spoken when the Friend had opened him up, when an indelible brand was burned within him: He was the Son, the one who would receive the inheritance of a thousand kings and then share it with all of us, everywhere. He was the Son who was loved, the Son who would love.

Many days later, the day the hunger returned, he fingered his ribs again, now lines of mountain ranges underneath his sunken chest, sensing the presence of someone or something. He looked behind him, then to his right, and finally to his left. His movements were languid. He hadn't eaten for so long that he'd forgotten how bread tasted. And then he looked down at his feet.

There was bread.

He could smell it, the flour and water and salt rising up into his mouth. And the thought came to him that if he reached down and took ahold of it, he would be full. For a few fleeting moments, his hand hung there, fingers outstretched, reaching for it. His eyes closed and suddenly he was surrounded by a grove of trees. He gasped. They filled him with a kind of longing that felt both familiar and utterly foreign. His arm remained reaching out, only this time it wasn't for bread; it was for fruit. It was then he realized that he wasn't alone. A thought floated into his mind suggesting that if he didn't eat that fruit, he would die.

When he opened his eyes, he had returned to the wilderness, to the bread by his feet. *There it is*, he thought, as he smiled.

Bread for the hungry. The words poured into him and then out of him. He knew where he was and what this was. This was a test.

> Remember the long way that the LORD your God
> has led you these forty years in the wilderness, in
> order to humble you, testing you to know what
> was in your heart, whether or not you would keep
> his commandments. He humbled you by letting
> you hunger, then by feeding you with manna,
> with which neither you nor your ancestors were
> acquainted, in order to make you understand that
> one does not live by bread alone, but by every word
> that comes from the mouth of the LORD.
>
> DEUTERONOMY 8:2-3

Not for the first time, he experienced a kind of filling that satisfied him, though his belly remained empty. He stared at the bread by his feet and was filled with something else, something wholesome. He knew it was the Friend; he smiled. He felt his belly and pulled at the stretchy skin. He looked at his knees, now knobby, bruised from falling on the rocks. He thought about his own body, warm to the touch in the desert sun.

"It's like bread," he mused. And then he thought about how his own blood had flowed on the rock. It was dark, like wine. My body and my blood.

After that, he was tired, so he crawled into his cave and slept. When he awoke, the sun was setting over the rocks and the shadows stretched out long under the endless sky. He liked to walk when the moon was high and the air was cold. He looked up at the stars, wheeling across the universe, giving direction to wanderers, to sailors. He found a large boulder and sat down. He shivered, but this time it wasn't the temperature. He was frightened.

His mind quickly turned to Abba, the one who had given him breath and also instructions, the one to whom he was utterly bound, in every way. But for the first time, he felt constricted by those bonds. He felt limited, powerless, and weak. Anger floated around the edges of his mind, seeping in. He was lost in the wilderness, where the Friend had led him. He was hungry.

And then a thought broke into his mind, like a stone hurled through a window.

I will give you authority. I will give you freedom to choose to do what you want to do.

You will be free to get married and experience the pleasure of a woman. Free to put down the burden of the world, which you carry on your back every waking moment. Free to live a quiet life. Free to say no to Abba. Free to look into the eyes of your children and see yourself staring back at you. Free to farm the land and grow old.

He wept for that woman, for that burden, and for that land. For a moment, he held it in his mind. He lingered on it, as if it were a meal laid out for him, its aroma filling his nostrils.

He fell, weakened by hunger and by the power of this longing. He stretched out his arms, palms flat on the ground, knees scraping rock. And then he noticed he was in a posture of supplication.

And then an ancient question broke the dream wide open.

"What will you bring with you?"

And he knew that he wanted only one particular kind of freedom, the one that bound him to Abba, because Abba was home. The Friend, Abba—they filled the loneliest places inside of him in ways that nothing and no one else did. That's what he brought with him.

And he knew the place that he was going, the place of promise, the place he would lead others to enter. He knew that was the only true choice for him. He knew that Abba had led him to this point. He knew that Abba had cared for his people, had rescued them from slavery, and would rescue them again. And he knew that freedom to choose to do what he wanted wasn't freedom at all if it meant freedom without Abba.

When GOD, your God, ushers you into the land he
promised through your ancestors Abraham, Isaac,
and Jacob to give you, you're going to walk into
large, bustling cities you didn't build, well-furnished
houses you didn't buy, come upon wells you didn't
dig, vineyards and olive orchards you didn't plant.
When you take it all in and settle down, pleased and
content, make sure you don't forget how you got
there—GOD brought you out of slavery in Egypt.

Deeply respect GOD, your God. Serve and worship
him exclusively.   DEUTERONOMY 6:10-13, MSG

At night, he walked under the moon. During the days,
he slept. His hair was tangled and his beard matted, and he
smelled. His fingernails were jagged and covered in dirt. His
feet were cut and bound with rags. He became aware of his
own suffering, his body dying. His digestive system had shut
down. His urine, in the rare times that it flowed, was brown,
the color of the Jordan River. His heart had slowed to a faint
murmur.

He fell back, stretched out his arms on each side, palms
upward, and closed his eyes. He heard shouts all around him,
angry accusations. His head burned, as if pierced by a ring
of fire. He couldn't move. He gasped with pain and from
lack of breath. The rags that barely covered him fluttered in
the breeze. His hands were claws. His heart was broken. He
looked down and saw shadowy figures by his feet. He tried
to focus on them, but his eyes failed.

For the third time in the wilderness, he knew he was not alone.

Jump down off this place of pain and destruction. Abba will surely catch you and take away your misery.

Words poured out of his mouth, a revolutionary bark that came from somewhere deep within. "Do not put the LORD your God to the test as you did at Massah" (Deuteronomy 6:16, NIV).

His body was a shell at this point, a rock. And suddenly he was surrounded by a group of people. He was aware of their fear and their thirst. A man was standing on a rock with a staff in his hand. He suddenly struck the rock with that staff, and a loud crack pierced the air. Water poured out of the rock, and all the people clamored around to drink it. It was then that he felt the water flowing from his side, mixed with blood.

And all was quiet.

It is finished, Jesus thought as he got up off the ground and slowly walked out of that wilderness toward home.

———•———

It's jarring to think about Jesus starving in the wilderness, face-to-face with Satan. It's upsetting to think of Jesus as weak, frail. We prefer to think of him as a superhero, swatting temptations as if they were flies and then marching back to Galilee to do the real work.

Richard Rohr wrote this about the nature of Jesus in the wilderness:

We like to imagine that Jesus did not flinch, doubt, or ever question God's love. The much greater message is that in his humanity he *did* flinch, have doubts, and ask questions—and still remained faithful. He is indeed our "pioneer and perfecter" in the ways of faith, who "disregards the shamefulness of it all" (see Hebrews 12:2).[1]

The word translated as "pioneer" is the Greek word *archegos*, which means "one who takes the lead in anything and so provides an example; a predecessor; a pioneer." An *archegos* starts something so that others may someday follow. When a ship crashes into the rocks, an *archegos* ties a rope onto herself, jumps into the dangerous water, and swims to shore so that the others on the ship can follow the rope to safety.[2]

The writer of Hebrews described Jesus like this:

Now that we know what we have—Jesus, this great High Priest with ready access to God—let's not let it slip through our fingers. We don't have a priest who is out of touch with our reality. He's been through weakness and testing, experienced it all—all but the sin. HEBREWS 4:14-15, MSG

Jesus was fully divine, but the way Jesus took the lead in facing temptation was not by accessing that divinity like a bag of tricks but by accessing it with a very human dependence on the God who is enough—and who would go all the way with him.

The startlingly good news is that we can do the same when we find ourselves in the wilderness.

The first temptation—to turn stones into bread (Luke 4:3)—has to do with being hungry and stuffing our faces with non-nourishing things. We turn stones into bread every time we act as though a job or a marriage or a bestselling book or a promotion (or the new iPhone) will satisfy us at the soul level. Jesus knew that those things were good and sometimes even necessary, but they would never fill us where we are most hungry—we do not live by bread alone but by every word that comes out of the mouth of God.

If you're married, you've tried to turn your stone of a marriage into bread. Now don't get me wrong—if you have a good spouse, you have a great gift. But your marriage is the crucible through which you might finally learn to be less self-referential; it's not the Promised Land. If you treat your marriage as if it's the bread that will satisfy you on a deep soul level, you'll stay disappointed and starving.

I have another friend named Steve whom I run with most Wednesdays. He's a therapist, and we always dive right into the deep end of the pool when we talk. Yesterday, we were talking about marriage and how hard it is sometimes.

"You're a pastor," he said. "Do you know what a sacrament is?"

"Explain it to me," I responded, sensing that he wanted to tell me.

"Sacraments are symbols," Steve said, "that are meant to *point us* to the thing, but they themselves are *not the thing*. Marriage is a sacrament in the Catholic Church. And marriage is particularly tricky because it comes so close to giving us what we want, but in that closeness it also reveals how far away even that is. Our spouses can take us part of the way, but they can't go all the way with us. At some point, we need to face God with nothing but our true selves, because only God can bring us all the way to where we need to go."

Sacraments are good things, as far as they go. They just can't go all the way.

When I insist on trying to turn stones into bread, I'm like Cain, acquiring and possessing, and it's never enough. When I decide to wait, however, resisting the temptation to try to make something happen, I become a gentle breeze, like Abel. I give others—and God—more of my best because I'm not trying to conjure up something that isn't there.

The second temptation—when Satan offered to give Jesus authority (Luke 4:6; some translations use *dominion* or *power*)—is not quite what it seems to be. The word for "authority" is the Greek word *exousia*, which can mean quite a few things: "to have physical or mental power," "to have the kind of authority where people must obey you," or "to have great influence." But it also means "to have power of choice; to have the freedom to do what you please."

Jesus already had the kind of mental power that would later cause people to be amazed at his teaching. He would soon have great influence. But the freedom to choose to do anything he wanted to do in this big, wide world? He could have grown old, gotten married, and had kids. He wouldn't have gone to the cross.

He could have had a *normal* life.

He could have escaped his calling, his *actual* life. Again, I think we prefer a Jesus who wasn't really tempted by this, who aced these temptations because he saw the cheat sheet beforehand. But I'm more in love with a Jesus who actually *was* tempted to walk away from God and have a normal life but *didn't*. Aren't you? Instead of choosing to lead himself, he kept choosing to be led by God.

What do you do when you want to escape your actual life? What fantasies do you spin when you want to leave your life and just do what you *want* to do? When I'm feeling especially entitled to an easier life, I stack up reasons why I deserve something other than what's in front of me. The choice Jesus made to keep worshiping God—to keep being led by God—is the countercultural, lonely decision to be the person God made you to be, no matter where it leads you.

Jesus' third temptation—when Satan brought him to the top of the Temple and told him to jump off because angels would surely catch him before he hurt himself (see Luke 4:9-11)—is about doing something spectacular to prove you are who you say you are.[3] From the top of the Temple, Jesus would be visible to every religious leader—everyone who will go on to question his identity for the next three years. Why not do something amazing that removes all doubt he's the Son of God?

I know what it's like to try to be spectacular. I know what it's like to try to prove myself, over and over and over again. When I published my first book, I imagined all the spectacular comments, invitations, and praise that would come pouring in. And when they didn't, at least not as many as I would have liked, I realized that I was trying to turn my stone of a book into bread. It's a good stone! It just isn't good bread.

The wilderness is the place where your false self is revealed. Your false self is your ego self. It's endlessly self-referential, clamoring for attention and success. Your ego self is important, but it doesn't know what you need. The wilderness is the place where your false self can starve so that your true self can emerge and be fed.

The wilderness offers you a chance to find out what's really inside of you, the ordinary stuff beneath your false self, which is so preoccupied with answering those temptations with hubris and self-propelled energy. The wilderness offers you a chance to *stop yourself.* Turning stones into bread is exhausting. Fantasizing about escaping your actual life is discouraging. And trying to be spectacular all the time is dehumanizing.

The wilderness offers a paradoxical gift: When you have been disappointed enough by the mirages that the false self creates, a beautiful simplicity comes into view, an ordinary oasis where you can rest and drink. You find out what you really want and that you actually can *receive* it. And when you do, it's actually satisfying.

At a particularly low point while I was writing this book,

I found myself exhausted and depressed. I had been working hard meeting writing deadlines, publishing a weekly podcast and a blog, performing my duties as a pastor at a two-year-old church plant, and trying to be a good husband and father. I was striving to be successful at all those things, and I didn't feel very successful at any of them. My false self was starving and demanding.

During that time, I sensed an invitation from God to take a break from my public self so I could gain more access to my private self. I talked to some friends and to Mary about how I was feeling and what I might be able to do about it. We all decided that for forty days I would stop all blogging, the podcast, and all social media. I needed to stop doing all those things because they can easily become ways in which I try to be spectacular, ways in which I can prove myself as worthy if I get enough likes or listens or retweets.

After a few weeks of that wilderness, a new awareness began to grow in me. I found myself able to be more present with my actual feelings and with people. When I stopped cranking out content, I became aware of the things in my life for which I felt grateful.

My three rascally boys.

The taste of really good coffee.

My friend Kyle, who makes me laugh and who loves me so well.

The people at my church.

My wife, Mary, and how she makes ordinary things in our family so special.

Great novels.

The sunrise.

The feeling of my legs moving over the pavement on a long run.

God.

In the wilderness, you're given the opportunity to be sustained by the God who will go all the way with you, no matter how hungry you get. No matter how weak, how frail, or how lost. It's the place where you learn you're not all that impressive, and you don't need to be. It's the place where you learn the ordinary you is enough. The wilderness offers you a chance to be restored by God, if you will stay there long enough.

A few words about what it feels like to be in the wilderness:

Your normal way of life doesn't work anymore.

One of my favorite wilderness stories is found in Numbers 11, in which the children of Israel were sick of manna (a kind of bread that God provided for them in the wilderness every morning). They wanted meat. They fondly remembered the fish they used to eat in Egypt (when they were slaves), along with the cucumbers, melons, leeks, onions, and garlic. When you're in the wilderness, it's easy to think that Egypt wasn't really all that bad. So they complained to Moses, and Moses went to God and lost it.

> Why have you treated your servant so badly? . . . Did I
> conceive all this people? Did I give birth to them, that
> you should say to me, "Carry them . . . to the land

that you promised . . . ?" . . . I am not able to carry all
this people alone, for they are too heavy for me. If this
is the way you are going to treat me, put me to death
at once. NUMBERS 11:11-12,14-15

Moses had been leading the children of Israel for about a
year, and it had been hard. But he got to a place where he just
couldn't do it anymore. The wilderness is where you are when
nothing seems to be working and you're not sure how to fix it.

Your dig-deep button seems to be broken.
You've tried to white-knuckle it. You've tried to prove that
you're bigger than your vices. You're exhausted and hungry.
You're lonely and you feel as though you're never going to
feel any different, ever. You're probably moving slow, and you
need lots more sleep. You wonder why you can't do as much
as you used to. You're cranky.

Have you ever stared at a kitchen sink full of dishes and
felt as though you just couldn't possibly face them? As if there
were no amount of money in the world that would motivate
you to wash them? The wilderness is the place where you're
invited to walk away from the dig-deep button and find a
more sustainable way of living.

Something deep and true about you is being brought to the surface.
In Deuteronomy 8:2-3, the children of Israel are reminded
what happened to them during those forty long years of wandering in the wilderness:

Remember every road that GOD led you on for
those forty years in the wilderness, pushing you
to your limits, testing you so that he would know
what you were made of, whether you would keep
his commandments or not. He put you through
hard times. He made you go hungry. Then he fed
you with manna, something neither you nor your
parents knew anything about, so you would learn
that men and women don't live by bread only;
we live by every word that comes from GOD's
mouth. (MSG)

A test from God is not to reveal how defective you are;
it's to reveal what's already inside of you, and even what's
lacking, so God can provide it for you. The children of Israel
got hungry, so they cried out to God to feed them. And God
gave them manna. And when they faced the existential loss
of identity while wandering for forty years, God refreshed
them and helped them live "by every word that comes from
GOD's mouth."

At the end of the day, what we need in the wilderness is a
deep sense of connection with God, a word that will help us
face the temptation to make something happen on our own,
or help us leave our actual lives and our calling, or help us
be spectacular.

God has met me a few times in my life with words so
powerful that they have changed my trajectory. One of those
times happened right after I left that big church to start

Genesis, when I tried to turn lots of stones into bread and felt as though I had to be spectacular.

----•----

I met Marcos in Long Beach, California, at a training session for denominational pastors. Marcos was introduced to us as someone who had the gift of prophetic prayer and would be available for anyone who wanted to meet with him. If you didn't grow up in the church or in that kind of church, let me explain that "the gift of prophetic prayer" means Marcos is sometimes able to hear from God while praying with people and knows things about them that he couldn't know in any other way. So Marcos could sometimes hear from God for people and then bring God's message to them.

We called him "the prophet."

I believe in that kind of thing, as mysterious as it sounds. I noticed that quite a few pastors were meeting with him. I saw them huddled together, praying. I saw some of them crying, then hugging him. But I was afraid to meet with the prophet.

As the training went on, more than a few pastors asked me if I had met with the prophet. I kept feeling very resistant to meeting with him, though I wasn't really sure why. He seemed gentle, even quiet.

On the final morning, I sat by the pool with my journal, wrestling with whether I should meet with Marcos. I felt as though I should, but I just didn't want to. I finally realized that I didn't want to meet with the prophet because I was convinced that he would have a word from God for me, and that word was absolutely going to be that I was arrogant. I didn't want to hear that from God. I felt fragile and vulnerable. I didn't want to be confronted.

And then my friend Ricky Jakubowski found me by the pool.

"You have to meet with him," he said. "It was so crazy. I don't really believe in those kinds of things. I mostly met with him to prove that he was a fake. But it was crazy. What he said was right on the money."

So I finally met with the prophet. He asked me my name and why I wanted to meet with him. I honestly don't remember what I said. We closed our eyes and prayed. It was silent for a couple of minutes, and then he spoke.

"I'm getting this picture of Joseph and the coat his father gave him," he said.

Hot shame washed over me. I knew it.

Joseph was the arrogant brother who kept badgering his older brothers about the self-aggrandizing dreams he was having and about how they meant that one day he would rule over his brothers—which is an extremely rude thing to say to your older brothers, even if it's true.

Here it comes, I thought. *God is going to talk to me about my arrogance.*

The prophet opened his eyes and looked at me. "Why do you think his father gave him that coat?" he asked.

I remained silent.

"He gave it to him to *honor* him. I think God wants you to know that he is going to honor you."

I'm not really a person who cries very much. I have nothing against crying. Sometimes I even *try* to cry. But I just end up making those odd whimpering sounds, as though the cry is caught somewhere in my throat and doesn't want to come out.

But when Marcos said that God wanted to honor me, I lost it. I wept and wept as he prayed over me, whispering words of compassion and healing and love.

For someone who has been raised by Approval and Admiration, hearing that God *honored me* was a gentle breeze, a *racham* (compassion) that nourished me and caused something brand new to grow in me.

As I process my own brokenness, this word of *honor* causes me to *re-member* (to put back together that which had been scattered) the painful memories of my childhood with healing and compassion instead of self-condemnation. I can imagine Jesus coming to find me on that basketball court and gently pulling me off Jimmy, then listening to me as I pour out my loneliness and anger. I can imagine Jesus confronting the boys who were making fun of me through the window of that storage room where I sat with the speech therapist, and then him walking back over to me and sitting next to me as I stuttered my way through those exercises. And I can imagine Jesus sitting with me in the dugout, offering an ice cream cone and a hug, that day in sixth grade when I struck out four times.

I'm not sure what the name *Jesus* conjures up for you.

Maybe it's the code word to get into an exclusive club filled with people with whom you'd rather not spend five minutes.

Maybe it reminds you of scary sermons and creepy crucifixes from your childhood.

Maybe you hear it and you're encouraged—because Jesus loves you, this you know—but not *too* encouraged because Jesus loves *everybody*: He has to; it's his job.

Maybe you're lost in the wilderness and you don't know what you believe anymore.

What will you find when you wind up in the wilderness? What voices will try to silence you? And what voices will nourish you?

The wilderness is one of the main characters in the Hebrew Scriptures. Abraham, Jacob, Moses, and of course the entire Hebrew population all spend time there. The Hebrew word for "wilderness" is *midbar*. The word *midbar* derives from the same root as *dabar*, which means "to speak."

Whose voice will you hear in the wilderness?

Hagar (Abram's concubine who bore him Ishmael, his first son) is the first person to run to the wilderness in the Scriptures. She's Egyptian, and she hears the angel of the Lord speak to her (see Genesis 16:7-8) while she's sitting by a fountain of water. (Water? In the wilderness?) The angel asks where she's been and where she's going. She can only answer where she's been because she doesn't know where she's going. After this interaction, she gives God a name. She says,

"You are the God who sees me" (Genesis 16:13, NIV). She is experiencing radical vulnerability.

Moses spent most of his life in the wilderness (forty years before returning to Egypt and another forty with the children of Israel), and in my opinion, that is why he's called the most humble man on earth (see Numbers 12:3).

The children of Israel spent forty years in the wilderness after leaving Egypt. I guess that's how long it took to get Egypt out of them.

And of course Jesus spent forty days in the wilderness.

You will end up in the wilderness more than once in your life. And when you do, I hope you find comfort in knowing that the wilderness is the place where God speaks. In my own wilderness journey recently, God has been replacing Approval and Admiration with Compassion and Intimacy. I'm finding them to be much better guides for me in the second half of my life.

The wilderness is a womb in which mercy can grow, if you let it. And when it grows, you can offer it to those who are overcome with shame and regret.

When you finally leave the wilderness, you will not be the same person who entered it, as long as you let it do what it needs to do: starve the false self and nourish the true self. There *are* things that need to change in me; they just won't be changed by feeling bad about myself or trying really hard to fix them. That isn't how wholeness works. The journey of wholeness is not a self-improvement project. It's a journey of loss, trust, transformation, and eventually hope.

When you've done your work in the wilderness, it's time to *inhabit* the land flowing with milk and honey. It's time to cross over into Canaan, the Promised Land.

But you have to see it to enter it.

*May you hear the compassionate voice of God calling
to you as you suffer in the wilderness. May you
smell the fragrance of freedom as you leave behind
the narrow place. And may you see the horizon
of the Promised Land coming slowly into view.*

QUESTIONS *for Reflection & Discussion*

1. This chapter opens with a raw and surprising story of what it might have been like for Jesus in the wilderness. What feelings rose up in you as you read that?

2. What are the stones in your life that you keep trying to turn into bread?

3. "You can't experience wholeness without experiencing the wilderness." Do you agree or disagree? Why?

4. Do you think God tests people? If so, why do you think God tests them? If you don't think God tests people, what is your reasoning?

5. "Christ is the bread," Augustine wrote, "awaiting hunger." What are you really hungry for these days? Be as specific and honest as you can. Don't worry about giving the right answer. Just give the real answer.

THE PROMISED LAND

*It was the Unicorn who summed up what everyone was feeling. He
stamped his right fore-hoof on the ground and neighed, and then cried:
"I have come home at last! This is my real country! I belong here. This is
the land I have been looking for all my life, though I never knew it till
now. The reason why we loved the old Narnia is that it sometimes looked
a little like this. Bree-hee-hee! Come further up, come further in!"*

The Last Battle, THE CHRONICLES OF NARNIA

MOSES CLIMBED ALL the way to the top of Mount Nebo
with a potency that defied his 120 years. From that vantage
point, he saw the ramparts of Jericho glistening in the late
afternoon sun. He slumped down on a large rock, breathing heavily, rubbing his tired legs with his strong hands. He
closed his eyes, remembering, and saw the palace in which he
had been raised; the surprised look on the Egyptian's face—
the one he had murdered—as the man lay dying in the sand;
the well in the wilderness where he had met his wife for the
first time; and the bush and the dancing flames, when everything changed.

And then suddenly he saw *so much more*.

It all spread out before him, much farther than the eye could see: Dan in the distant north, the Negev in the south, and the Great Sea to the west. He was seeing the Promised Land—the land of the sons of Israel that had been promised to Abram all those years ago. He was seeing *all* of it, though he would never enter.

He smiled, remembering all the twists and turns of his remarkable life. He had known God face-to-face, and the moment he saw the Promised Land stretched out before him, he knew that he had already been carrying the Promised Land in his heart for a very long time. He would soon enter a different kind of Promised Land, the very best kind.

He was at rest for the first time in his long life.

Moses was buried in a valley in the land of Moab, but it's not clear who buried him, and no one knows the site of his burial. Legend has it that it was God who buried Moses, a fitting end for the most humble man on the earth.

The children of Israel wept for thirty days when Moses died.

Not long after the mourning period was over, Joshua shivered in the early morning hours before the sun came up. It was springtime and still very cold. He walked to the Jordan River and watched as the water spilled over its banks. He stood on the very edge of the wilderness. On the other side of the Jordan was the Promised Land.

He scratched his long beard as tears leaked out of his leathery eyes. Not very many weeks ago, Moses had laid those powerful hands on Joshua's shoulders and anointed him as the new leader of the children of Israel. Electricity had passed between them in that moment, nearly knocking Joshua to the ground. Moses would die, and Joshua would lead them into the Promised Land.

Here I am, Joshua thought.

As the sound of the rushing waters of the Jordan filled his ears, he remembered how the Voice had told him what to do.

Arise. Lead the people across the Jordan, into the land that I am giving to them. Every single place the sole of your foot will walk upon in that land, I have already given you. Just as I was with Moses, so I will be with you. I will never fail you, and I will never leave you. Be strong and courageous. I am with you wherever you go.[1]

Joshua swallowed hard and looked around. The sun's fingers were just stealing over the mountain, which meant that soon the camp would be stirring. When he heard a baby's cry pierce the morning air, he walked toward *his* people. For the briefest of moments, he wavered. Did the Voice really say that God would be with him wherever he went? The river at springtime was raging, wild; how many would die as they crossed the river? Was it worth it?

The trumpets blared as the priests went first, as God had instructed them to, carrying the Ark of the Covenant toward the river. Sweat trickled down the napes of their necks, but even as the water covered their ankles, they kept walking.

Joshua held his breath as he watched. Suddenly he realized the weight that Moses had carried all those years. How had he done it? What had carried him as he carried the people?

And then the raging river stopped flowing. The water coming from upstream piled up into a wall, and the water running downstream simply flowed away. And that is how the children of Israel crossed over. Just as he had at the Red Sea forty years before, God provided a way through what seemed impossible.

When everyone had crossed over, they camped on the east border of Jericho at a place called Gilgal, where they took twelve stones—representing each of the tribes of Israel—and piled them as a monument to God's faithfulness, telling the story of a crossing over from death to new life in the land God had promised them so many years ago.

The grandfathers all wept for their dead fathers, who were buried in the wilderness. They wept for their sons, who were armed for battle, getting ready to attack Jericho. And they wept for joy for their grandchildren, who would grow up in a spiritual community that had finally found its home.

It's one thing to finally escape the barren wilderness. It's another thing entirely to return home.

—•—

You won't stay in the wilderness forever.

Let that soak in for a moment.

More than once in your life, you will be asked to leave

what you know to go to a place God will show you. You're on a continual journey from here to there. We're not meant to be border keepers; we're meant to be border crossers. God causes us to see something new, and when we have the courage to cross over, our borders expand and move with us.

I saw this happen in my relationship with my associate pastor Steve after our conflict.

When my relationship with Steve began to heal, it was tentative at first. We were both raw and bruised. But it didn't take very long to realize that we weren't in the wilderness anymore. We had crossed over into a new way of believing in each other, guarding each other, and trusting each other. We think about our friendship—and ourselves—differently now. We have crossed over into a new way of relating. We haven't arrived—there's still so much more to see and know about each other. But we have moved from here to there.

Catie's emergence from a lifetime of self-loathing was very slow in coming. It was as if she kept trying on new identities to see if they would fit. It was uncomfortable at first. But she kept saying things such as "The old me would have been wounded by that small comment, and it would have taken me out for days, maybe weeks. But it doesn't affect me like that anymore. I'm changing!" She sees differently. She has crossed over from here to *there*, into a new way of thinking and relating with herself, with God, and with others, and it's unmistakable. She hasn't arrived; she's still growing. But she has definitely moved from here to there.

What is the Promised Land, and how do you know when

you're there? Is it a geographical place, or is it an idea? Is it for now or for later? Or both? Who is it for?

Have you ever found yourself sitting across the table from someone you never thought you'd be with in the same room again?

Have you ever realized that you were alive again, after a long season of what felt like dying?

Have you ever almost lost someone, but at the last minute, he or she was saved?

Have you ever almost lost yourself, but at the last minute, you were saved?

Have you ever been offered genuine forgiveness?

Have you ever been the one to offer genuine forgiveness?

Have you ever smelled the sweet fragrance of a second or third or tenth chance?

Have you ever suddenly realized that you're no longer *on the way* there, but you're actually there?

If so, you have inhabited the Promised Land.

A few weeks ago, I was sitting in church listening to Steve preach, and he was killing it. Steve brought us into a new place of seeing what a life of wholeness—as a community—could look like.

"I have to apologize to you all," he said. "I have worked in the church for a very long time, but I am just recently seeing what a life of peace really looks like. And I don't know exactly what our next step is, but what compels me to share is that we have a hope, and that hope is stronger, more beautiful, and better than anything we see in the world today."

It was just a sermon—but I got a brief glimpse of what the church could look like in the world twenty years from now, and it looked radiant. I felt so motivated to help him, to give him whatever resources, encouragement, and prayer he needs so that he can lead people there. And I thanked God for the transforming work of reconciliation that had happened between the two of us. It felt like the Promised Land. I believe that I was seeing the sacred future; I believe that we're on the way *there*.

We understand the word *Hebrew* to refer to a group of people (the Israelites) and also to a language. But in the Scriptures, the word *Hebrew*—in biblical Hebrew—is one of the most fascinating I've ever come across.

It's first used in Genesis 14:13 to describe Abram the Hebrew (*ivri*). *Ivri* means "one from beyond" or "from the other side." The related verb form *aver* means "to pass, cross, traverse, or undergo." To be Hebrew essentially means to cross over.

The Promised Land isn't about getting everything you want, nor does it mean you stop moving. It's not about being conflict-free or finding out the grass *is* actually greener there.

The Promised Land is home to anyone who has left Egypt, passed through the fires of transformation in the wilderness, and crossed over into an entirely different place. It's about moving from here to there. It's about crossing over.

So let's talk about where "there" is.

Before Joshua crossed over into the Promised Land, when God spoke to him so tenderly and with such strength, God showed him what the Promised Land actually is. God also told Joshua to "be strong and courageous" *three times* in nine verses (Joshua 1:1-9). He told Joshua that he would never leave or fail him and that he'd already given Joshua every place that the soles of his feet would walk upon.

The Promised Land is not a cure-all for everything that has gone wrong previously in our lives. If that were true, the words that God gave to Joshua wouldn't make any sense. We don't need to be strong and courageous to drink milk and eat honey all day.

We don't even need God in order to do that.

Joshua walked to Jericho soon after he crossed over, and he found it to be a heavily fortified city that seemed invincible, another impassable Red Sea to cross. There he met a powerful man holding a sword, and Joshua immediately confronted the man. He was ready for a fight.

> Once when Joshua was by Jericho, he looked up and
> saw a man standing before him with a drawn sword
> in his hand. Joshua went to him and said to him,
> "Are you one of us, or one of our adversaries?" He
> replied, "Neither; but as commander of the army of
> the LORD I have now come." And Joshua fell on his
> face to the earth and worshiped, and he said to him,
> "What do you command your servant, my lord?" The
> commander of the army of the LORD said to Joshua,
> "Remove the sandals from your feet, for the place
> where you stand is holy." And Joshua did so.
>
> JOSHUA 5:13-15

The Hebrew Scriptures are written with a brilliant story-telling method that I like to call "leaving a thread to pull." In Joshua 5:13, the Hebrew phrase *nasa ayin* is translated as "he looked up and saw," which means "to lift up, carry, or bear (*nasa*) your eyes (*ayin*)." When you pull the thread in Joshua 5:13, it leads you to Genesis 13:14-17, where the exact same phrase (*nasa ayin*) is used when God tells Abram to raise his eyes and see the Promised Land that would exist in the future.

> The LORD said to Abram, after Lot had separated from him, "Raise [*nasa*] your eyes [*ayin*] now, and look from the place where you are, northward and southward and eastward and westward; for all the land that you see I will give to you and to your offspring forever. I will make your offspring like the dust of the earth; so that if one can count the dust of the earth, your offspring also can be counted. Rise up, walk through the length and the breadth of the land, for I will give it to you."

The writer is not so subtly hinting that what's happening *now* in the Promised Land with Joshua is very closely associated to what was happening *then* in the Land of Canaan with Abram.

The promise that God had given Abram is now finally being fulfilled with Joshua.

So we know the promise is being fulfilled, but we still

have to deal with the dangerous man with a drawn sword standing in between Joshua and Jericho. Who is this man, why has he drawn a sword, and how should Joshua respond?

Joshua is standing face-to-face with this man—opposite, or in front of him. It looks like a classic showdown. The Hebrew word for "opposite" or "in front of" is *neged*. *Neged* also refers to a counterpart or a mate; someone who stands eye-to-eye with you, before your face. This is another beautiful thread that is begging to be pulled.

The first usage of a form of the word *neged* is in Genesis 2:18, when the woman (Eve) is created to stand face-to-face with the man (Adam). "The LORD God said, 'It is not good for the man to be alone. I will make a helper suitable for him'" (NIV).

"Suitable helper" is a pretty weak translation to describe the first woman, especially when you think of how strong and powerful women are. The Hebrew phrase that is translated as "suitable helper" is *ezer kenegdo*.[2] *Ezer* does mean "help," but it's usually only used to describe the kind of strong, powerful, and lifesaving help that God gives (see Psalm 20:2; 33:20; 70:5; and 115:9). *Kenegdo* means "face-to-face" or "opposite," as it is formed from the word *neged*.

But Joshua isn't seeing it. He asks, "Are you one of us, or one of our adversaries?" (Joshua 5:13). Joshua's question is understandable but almost comical. It's swaggering and proud, and I can almost see Joshua fingering his own sword, deciding if he will chop off this man's head right then or if he'll wait until after he has answered.

"Neither," the man answers.

What?

The man with the sword would either be his adversary or his ally, depending on how Joshua saw him. If Joshua insisted on taking Jericho by himself, because he was the *leader*, God would indeed be an adversary.

Instead Joshua fell to his feet in worship (verse 14), when he was seeing that the man with the drawn sword was a representative of God, an ally who had come to stand face-to-face (*neged*) with him as he saw to the fulfillment of his task now that he was *inside* the Promised Land. Joshua's task was to prepare a place where the next generation of the children of Israel could be at home at last.

The Promised Land is about inhabiting sacred space, where you have crossed over from a life of hiding, blaming, and scapegoating to a life of seeing that God's presence and provision really are enough as you go about the unique ways in which you bring shalom to your brothers and sisters.

We read over and over again that it's a land flowing with milk and honey. Milk is provision, and honey is presence. The Promised Land is the place where you see and experience God's continual provision for you (milk) and God's continual presence with you (honey). Milk nourishes us, and God's presence sweetens life. That's what Moses experienced on Mount Nebo. He didn't need to enter the Promised Land because he had already experienced it.

You're inhabiting the Promised Land when you see that God has called you to raise those three kids and that God is with you in that task and will never fail you—even though you sometimes want to hide in the pantry and eat five pounds of chocolate and never come out. You are a mother. You are a father. Be strong and courageous. God will give you what you need.

You're inhabiting the Promised Land when you see that you can keep returning to teaching in that difficult classroom because God is with you. And God will never fail you, even though you sometimes feel sick with dread on Sunday nights just thinking about Monday morning. You are a teacher. Be strong and very courageous. God will give you what you need.

You know you're in the Promised Land when you receive face-to-face companionship and lifesaving help from God to do the task that is yours to do.

You know you're in the Promised Land when you have whispered your secret for how you want to change the world and you are given powerful, lifesaving help to get it done.

You know you're in the Promised Land when you find yourself preparing a place for other weary travelers stuck in Egypt or wandering in the wilderness to someday drink milk (nourishment) and taste honey (sweetness) from God.

Which brings me to the barn swallows.

———•———

A few years ago, some birds showed up and began building a nest in a little alcove under our front porch. I didn't know anything about these birds, other than how many droppings they could produce, so I pulled a ladder from the garage and took their nest down. *Problem solved*, I thought. When Mary and the boys realized what I had done, they may or may not have hated me for a rather unfair amount of time. They told me that the birds were barn swallows, that they were monogamous, and that they returned year after year to the same place to lay their eggs. I had just destroyed their home.

"But . . . I mean, the poop," I complained.

I was heavily outnumbered, and I lost that battle.

A few weeks later, those stubborn barn swallows had rebuilt their nest, and because I was banned from touching it, they laid their first clutch of eggs. While Mary and the kids went out every morning to check the progress, I muttered profanities under my breath as I saw the droppings that were covering our porch.

They watched the eggs, and I cleaned up the droppings.

When the eggs hatched, half a dozen fuzzy little birds peered down at us. After a week or so, those fuzzy little birds courageously left the nest and flew away. I'm told those same birds will sometimes return to the nest to help their parents tend to the next clutch of eggs. Barn swallows lay two clutches of eggs every year, which means lots of birds and lots of droppings.

One day, Ben came in from the front yard, crying. "Daddy, one of the baby birds has something wrong with its wing. It can't fly. We have to help it."

I went outside with Ben and saw the little bird struggling

on the grass. One of its wings was deformed; it would never fly. It kept trying and trying, but it wasn't going anywhere. Ben cried and cried.

Those little barn swallows have carved out a place in our hearts. We look forward to their return to our house every year and watch their fuzzy heads closely when it comes time for them to fly the nest. Most of the time, we wake up and they're just gone. But sometimes we find one or two lying dead on the concrete floor of the porch, and I gently scoop them up. Or we find that a predator has swooped in and eaten them. But those barn swallows keep returning home every summer, and they keep laying their eggs. We keep watch over them. We guard them. And of course we clean up their poop.

It turns out that swallows are highly symbolic birds. Because swallows always return to the same place to nest every year, sailors in the early days would get a tattoo of a swallow before the journey began and then get another one after they had safely returned. Swallows also represent affection between family members and friends and their loyalty in always returning to them.

The ceramic bird on the cover of this book is a swallow. Its fifteen broken pieces you see at the top were sent to Des Metzler, a professional ceramic restorer in South Africa. It was missing some shards, but he fully restored it to the condition you see at the bottom of the cover.[3] When the publishers sent us the cover art, they had no idea of our love story with the barn swallows. I smiled and decided their story had to become a part of this book.

Partnering with God in doing your unique task in the Promised Land is mostly about learning to see what keeps returning home to you, making nests under your porch.

When you see it, your work is to create a safe place for it to make a nest so that it can give birth to new life in the world. Figuring out your secret—how you want to change the world—is mostly about paying attention to the barn swallows in your life that just won't go away and resisting the urge to tear down their nests. That will mean cleaning up some messes and cheering them on as they grow. It will sometimes mean crying when they don't make it.

My friend Kyle recently told me about a time in his childhood when his cousin Dan stayed with his family after Dan's brother had just died. One day, Dan holed himself up in Kyle's room and lost control. He was shouting and throwing things, raging. Kyle was afraid, so he found his mom, and she could see the fear in his eyes. But she was a wise woman, one who knew what it means to watch over those in her care.

"If it's okay with you," she told Kyle, "I think we should let Dan break all the stuff he wants to break. It's just stuff. A world of pain is trapped inside of him, and it needs to get out."

Kyle agreed, and Dan raged on. It's a wise person who knows how to guard another person. Shalom sometimes looks like allowing the pain to flow out unabated and unedited. Kyle is now a pastor of congregational care. He's one of the best people I know at guarding the souls of others.

We see a beautiful example of tending to those who return

to your nest in one of Jesus' most famous parables—the one about the Prodigal Son, his recklessly generous father, and his irritated older brother. This younger son had demanded that his father give him his inheritance early, and after he left and wasted it all, he returns home, hoping to be accepted as a slave in his father's house. His father throws a feast for him and gives him back his identity as a beloved son. But the older son storms outside, angry that all his years of getting it right appear to have been a waste of time. When the father comes out to talk to him, he says, "Son, you are always with me, and all that is mine is yours" (Luke 15:31).

I wonder what might have happened with Cain, the one who murdered Abel, if he had believed that he was always with God and all God had was his. When Cain withheld his best, I wonder if it was for the same reason that the older brother withheld his? They were both responsible, respectable sons. And they both missed out on the gift of God's presence and provision.

Thirty-nine years before Joshua entered the Promised Land, he would have been one of many Israelites who knelt to receive a blessing from the priests, as these familiar words from Numbers 6:24-26 were spoken over them:

> The LORD bless you and keep [*shamar*] you;
> the LORD make his face to shine upon you, and be
> gracious to you;
> the LORD lift up [*nasa*] his countenance upon you, and
> give you peace [*shalom*].

The metaphor of the swallows is deep and rich. It shows us what it means to guard and tend those who return home to us and build their nests under our protective covering. It shows us that we are birds ourselves, needing to be fed as babies in a nest by God's provision. It shows us what it looks like to return home to the Promised Land again and again, almost stubbornly. It shows us how to discern aspects of our calling—how to learn to see those ideas, people, longings, and experiences—that keep coming back, that won't leave us alone. And it shows us what it looks like to feed others, to clean up after others. The swallows teach us what it means to see to the shalom of our brothers and sisters, in all those ways and more.

Mary and I have made our nest around a large table of good friends, the kind with whom we let down our guards and the kind to whom we tell our secrets. It's Rick and Becky's table, and Micah and Laura join us. We eat delicious food. Sometimes Rick grills salmon fortified by his spice rub that he buys when traveling to various parts of the Middle East. Sometimes Micah boils, blanches, and flash-fries huge green beans, then dusts them with dill. There is always salad, bread, and vineyards of wine.

Glasses are filled and raised and filled again. Around Rick and Becky's table, you can't clink anyone's glass without looking in their eyes for at least two seconds. And you cannot pour your own wine. We offer the gift of wine to each other; it's almost Eucharistic. We laugh, we cry, and we tell our secrets to one another.

Laura usually asks a table question, which all of us

eventually answer, though it takes hours and hours. She has kind eyes, beautiful red hair, and a quiet strength that holds us all together.

We share provision and presence with one another.

One night around that table, someone asked me what I was going to name the new church we were planting.

"Genesis," I immediately answered. Though lots of things weren't obvious about church planting, the name always was. I wanted to create an environment in which people could experience new beginnings with God, with others, and with themselves.

Becky gasped and started weeping uncontrollably. She didn't stop for a very long time. When she finally could speak, she said, "I've been waiting my whole life to be a part of Genesis."

Becky is a strong woman, and many people build nests under her expansive care. We feel protective of her; we take special care of the nest she has built under our porch.

———

The borders of the Promised Land are crossed by those of us who are hungry for a future that is marked by wholeness instead of brokenness. It exists anywhere—and *anytime* people are living out the ancient idea of shalom in small or big ways. It exists anytime or anywhere shalom is planted, grown, and feasted on. You don't so much arrive in the Promised Land as you inhabit it, and it inhabits you.

*May you see the places where God is calling you
to cross over, and may you see that God will never
leave you or fail you. May you walk confidently,
knowing God will give you everything you need.*

QUESTIONS *for Reflection & Discussion*

1. How would you have described the Promised Land before reading this chapter?

2. What people, issues, or problems keep returning to you, and how do you think they relate to your secret—how you want to change the world?

3. What is a situation in your life right now in which you really need to hear God tell you that he is with you and will never fail you? Where do you need to be invited to be strong and courageous?

4. The Promised Land is about seeing that God is face-to-face (*neged*) with you, helping you walk out your unique task. In what ways have you experienced this? Are there situations where you feel as though you haven't?

5. How would you describe the Promised Land now?

EPILOGUE

Christel is the bread, awaiting hunger.

ST. AUGUSTINE

USUALLY, SEVEN MILES is a long way to walk, but there was nothing usual about our walk that day. We started in the city of Shalom—still burning with tension after Salvation had been executed—on our way to the village where the hot springs were. We needed to get away to process the razor blades of grief that had cut us wide open.

The waves of our conversation tossed and turned us so violently that we didn't even notice when a stranger approached and began to walk with us.

"What are you talking about?" he asked.

Something about how he asked his question broke that fresh wound wide open, and I couldn't speak. Cleopas

145

snapped at him, wondering how he hadn't heard about what had set Jerusalem on fire over the past three days. But then we told him about the cross, the empty tomb, and how some of our friends were hanging on to the desperate belief that Salvation might somehow be alive. Some of them went back to that tomb, but they didn't see anything.

And then the stranger started talking.

He talked about the Garden, the hiding, and the deception. He talked about Cain and Abel, about Jacob and Esau, and then he talked a lot about Joseph. He talked about the lost years in Egypt. He talked about Moses and the journey through the wilderness. He talked about Joshua and entering the Promised Land. He talked about King David, his son Solomon, and the rest of the kings—the wretched ones and the good ones. He talked about Elijah, Jeremiah, and Isaiah. He talked about John the Baptist and about Rome. He talked and talked and talked, and our hearts raced as he did.

When we arrived at the house where our friends were staying, we invited the stranger to share the evening meal. When he sat down at the table, he reached out and began ripping the bread apart with a lusty hunger and a familiar smile. Then he gave us the bread, and when he did, the two of us burst out laughing. How did we miss it? The others hid their eyes and wept, but we couldn't keep it in. He had been with us for miles, and we hadn't recognized him. It was almost as if we were birds in a nest; he just kept giving us the bread, and we just kept eating it.

And then he vanished right in front of us. He always was

a little slippery. But we weren't afraid anymore. Salvation had come back, and we couldn't get enough of him.

We still can't.

———•———

I wrote that story in the first person because the second disciple on the road to Emmaus isn't named, so it allows me to enter into the story myself. You can enter it too. We can walk with one another, and with Jesus, with all our questions, doubts, pain, and hopes—even the ones that have been dashed.

Joshua (*Yeshua*) means "salvation." *Jesus* (*Yeshua*) is the exact same word. Salvation will always lead you into the Promised Land, if you can recognize him (because sometimes he seems like a stranger at first). And then you will be fed by Salvation himself, where he is both the host *and* the meal at his own table of abundance.

After Joshua and the children of Israel crossed over into the Promised Land, they immediately shared the Passover meal. And the day after that, they ate the produce of the land. From then on, no manna ever appeared on the ground, but they ate the fruit of the Promised Land that year (see Joshua 5:10-12).

According to Luke's Gospel, Jesus—after he rose from the dead—shared a meal of bread and (we can assume) wine with those two friends in the small village of Emmaus.

It's fascinating that they only recognize Jesus over a meal.

There are so many meals in the Scriptures: Cain's vegetables and Esau's bowl of stew. There was manna in the wilderness, and there was the feeding of the five thousand. And who could forget the wedding at Cana when the water was turned into wine? All those meals point to a *final* meal—the Last Supper—the sacrament pointing to the real thing: that Jesus will go all the way with you, no matter how long your road is.

Jesus shared the Passover meal with his disciples on the night before he was betrayed, when he broke the bread of life and passed the cup of salvation. He told them—he told us—to keep sharing this meal together, and when they did—when we do—to remember him. Then he walked out into the dark night. He wept in the garden of Gethsemane. And later he was brought to a hill where he suffered and died, voluntarily, to see to the shalom of all of us, everywhere.

That meal—the Last Supper—is the nest we'll return to, over and over again, where we'll find both provision and presence. Some Christians call it Communion; others call it the Eucharist, Common Table, or Lord's Supper. It's a sacrament that helps us remember to return to Jesus, over and over again, for nourishment and sweetness.

Our church has cobbled together a liturgy for Eucharist from the Lutherans and the Episcopalians (we are Covenanters[1]—we can do that), and I love it. One of the things I love the most is the following statement. More than any sermon, more than anything else we do, people consistently comment on how they need to hear these words every single week:

This is the table, not of the church, but of the Lord.
It is made ready for those who love God and for
those who want to love God more. So come, you
who have much faith and you who have little; you
who have been here often and you who have not
been here long; you who have tried to follow and
you who have failed. Come, because it is the Lord
who invites you. It is God's will that those who want
God should meet God here.[2]

The Table of Salvation invites all who are hungry to come
and eat. The Table of Salvation restores that which is broken.
The Table of Salvation creates a sacred place of nourishment
where we come together bound not by common borders but
by common need.

I love the tradition the little ones began at our church,
though I'm not sure how it started. At the end of each service
(we receive the Eucharist every week), they gather around the
extra bread and juice, and they polish it off. It's messy and a
little crowded, but there's always enough to go around.

They can't get enough of it.

I realize that may seem highly sacrilegious to some, and
for that reason, I almost didn't mention it here. I don't mean
to offend anyone, and I certainly don't mean to make light
of something as significant as the Eucharist. But I think there
is something for us to learn from these kids, who greedily
gobble down that bread with abandon and do so without
concern for how they appear.

You will swallow your fair share of jagged glass in your life, and so will I. We'll spend a lot of time healing from our own mistakes and from the mistakes of others. As my friend Dave likes to say, we're all mixed bags. We need a home to return to, a safe place to be nourished.

On your journey toward wholeness, you'll hide and you'll be found again.

You'll worry that there isn't enough to go around, but you'll also give God the really good stuff.

You'll seek out some things that are horrible for you, but you'll see to the shalom of your brothers and sisters too.

You'll stubbornly stay in those familiar places for too long, but you'll eventually leave to go to the place God will show you.

You'll learn what your *etc* is, and then you'll forget it. Then you'll learn it again.

You'll get stuck in Egypt for too long, and Egypt will get stuck in you for even longer. You'll sometimes go back after you've already left. And sometimes you'll realize that you have become someone else's Egypt, and you'll weep tears of regret. And then God will hear your cries, and you'll be led through another Red Sea.

You'll eventually make your way into the wilderness, where temptation, heartache, and hunger will form something strong and true deep within you that will bless the world. And sometimes, you'll turn those stones into bread.

And then you'll try to bring others into the Promised Land, and you'll try to fix them instead of simply creating a space for them to build a nest. Or they'll try to fix you. Or they will refuse to enter in.

But you'll cross over into the Promised Land anyway, and you'll meet the man with the drawn sword, and you'll swagger, believing you have arrived and can do it on your own. But then you'll fall to your face and realize that God is your nourishment and your sweetness, and you can't be strong or courageous without him.

Then you'll hide again . . . and be found again . . .

See how it works? That's the journey of wholeness. Farther up and farther in.

So, my brothers and sisters, I'll leave you with a final benediction:

May you swallow the very bread of life, which has been broken for you. And may you drink the cup of salvation, which has been poured out for you. These are the gifts of God, given for the people of God, to see to our shalom. Take and eat.

GLOSSARY

Abel (Hebrew, noun): *a vapor or breeze.* The brother of Cain, who also murdered him (Genesis 4). Have you ever met people who feel like a gentle breeze when you're around them? They cool things down. They offer relief, refreshment. Abel offers God the firstborn of his flock—which is saying that he trusts God with his future, no matter what happens to his sheep. Abel shows us that it's possible to live outside of the Garden in radical and vulnerable trust. But Abel was murdered, showing us that living this kind of life is not a guarantee all will go well with you if you choose to trust God instead of your own ability to possess enough, to gain more and more (which is what *Cain* means). What do you do with that?

Archegos (Greek, noun): *the chief leader or prince; one who takes the lead in anything and thereby provides an example; a predecessor or pioneer.* Now this word, ladies and gentlemen, is so killer it makes me giddy. Taylor Swift is the *archegos* of teenage girls who have been hurt by boys but can shake it off anyway. Steve Jobs was the *archegos* of elegant smartphones enabling us to run businesses and take pictures and video-call our grandparents in Vermont. But Jesus is described as the *archegos* and finisher (*teleiotes*) of our *faith*. In the wilderness, on the cross, in the grave, and back to the Father and Spirit, Jesus blazed a trail of eternal life (which started at his resurrection) for us to follow. He is the true hero of the Hero's Journey.

Cain (Hebrew, noun): *to possess or to gain.* When Cain kills his brother, he offers us a picture of a person who gets lost in gaining personal success, which is the opposite representation of his brother, Abel, whose name means "vapor or gentle breeze." How many times in your life have you seen a gentle breeze get snuffed out by the spirit of possession or greed? The story of Cain and Abel is tragic because it happened to brothers, but we see it happening over and over again in ourselves and in our world.

Canaan (Hebrew, noun): *lowland.* The Promised Land is also called the Land of Canaan. *Canaan* is most likely related to the verb *cana*, which means "to be humbled," "to humble oneself," or "to kneel." I find it fascinating that the Promised Land is the place of humbling, the place where you kneel. Now, there's a wide debate among rabbis questioning whether *Canaan* is a Hebrew word or a Phoenician word. But if it's a Hebrew word, what does it mean that the land flowing with milk and honey is also the land of humbling?

Etc (Latin, adverb): *(et) and; (cetera) the other things.* I used *etc* in my surfing story as a metaphor to describe what you'll need to bring with you on your own journey of wholeness, "those extra things you're going to need that I can't even begin to tell you about, because it has to do with what's really essential for *you*; it's specific to what *you'll* need, and only *you* can discover what that is." In that embarrassing story, I realized I must leave behind my need to be awesome right away at everything and instead laugh more and begin to learn how to be a novice who is okay with looking stupid and not knowing.

Ezer Kenegdo (Hebrew): *Ezer* refers to help, but it's almost always used in the Scriptures as the lifesaving help that God gives to those who are desperate. *Kenegdo* means "to stand opposite" or "to be a counterpart or a mate, before one's face." My friend Shannon Staiger translates *ezer kenegdo* as "a strong, powerful, lifesaving help, a face-to-face companion, without which one would die." And that, my friends, is how Scripture describes the first woman when she is created by God. It's usually translated "suitable helper" or something like that, and that's unfortunate, to say the least.

Hineni (Hebrew, verb): *Here I am.* Possibly my favorite Hebrew phrase. It's always used as a *response* when someone's name is called. Moses answers "*hineni*" at the burning bush when God calls his name. Abraham answers "*hineni*" when God asks him to sacrifice his son Isaac. Samuel answers "*hineni*" when he thinks Eli is calling him at night. "*Hineni*" is a response that indicates a wholehearted commitment to being all in to whatever you're being called to do, even when you don't completely know what it is and even though you don't know what saying yes will entail. It's a response of radical trust and vulnerability. "*Hineni*" is what couples are saying to each other in their vows when they get married. "I don't know what's coming, I can't predict what this will cost, but I'm all in, with you, come what may." "*Hineni!*" It's Jesus' fundamental and first response to God throughout his entire life on earth.

Ivri (Hebrew, noun): *one from beyond; from the other side.* The verb form of *ivri* is *aver*, which means "to pass, cross, traverse, or undergo." It's first used in Genesis 14:13 to describe Abram the Hebrew (*ivri*). I find it fascinating that God's people are essentially named "those who come from the other side and cross over, traverse, or undergo something to get somewhere else." The people of God are a people who will cross over from one reality to another, in this life, and in the life to come. That inspires me.

Lech Lecha (Hebrew, verb + preposition + pronoun): *to go forth. Lech* means "go." When you add *lecha*, it personalizes the command. *Lecha* means "for you" or "to you." It's very personal and very challenging. It essentially means "Hey! I'm talking to *you*! Get yourself going!" Rashi (the great medieval commentator) understood *lech lecha* literally. He translated it as "go for you." Rashi wrote that the command means "Go for your own enjoyment and for your own good." He understood the command as an invitation to adventure and self-discovery. Where do you need to *lech lecha*, for the good of the world and for your own adventure and self-discovery?

Matsor (Hebrew, noun): *hindrance, limit, or restraint.* Remember, in Hebrew, a noun is a person, place, or thing *in action*. A job may be a *matsor* in your life that limits, hinders, or restrains you. *Matsor* can also be a good thing: The Whole 30 nutritional program is a *matsor* that limits your propensity to eat nachos and beer at 11 o'clock on a Tuesday night. *Matsor* is related to the word *Mitsrayim*, which is translated as *Egypt*. Egypt is the place that hindered, limited, and restrained the children of Israel for four hundred years.

Mitsrayim (Hebrew, noun): *Egypt. Mitsrayim* doesn't mean much until you take a look at the related word *matsor*, which comes from the same root meaning "to limit, hinder, or restrain." And suddenly Egypt is more than a geographical place. It's an emotional and spiritual state of being held captive, in slavery. What is your *Mitsrayim?* When we begin to learn to experience the Bible that way, we enter it instead of just reading it.

Nasa Ayin (Hebrew, verb + noun): *to lift up (nasa) your eyes (ayin).* It's a work of writing genius that the exact same phrase is used by Joshua when he looks up and sees the man with the drawn sword in Joshua 5:13 and by Abram when God causes him to see the future Promised Land in Genesis 13:14-17. The Promised Land is something that only God can cause us to see.

Neged (Hebrew, adverb): *the part opposite; specifically a counterpart or mate; before your face.* I wrote about this in chapter 8. When Joshua walks to Jericho, a man with a drawn sword, who is *neged* Joshua, confronts him. This is a powerful scene. Joshua is being given a counterpart, someone who will help him perform his task in the Promised Land, but Joshua seems to be so carried away by the moment that he doesn't see it. It's only when the man says he is neither adversary nor ally that Joshua sees that God is coming to help him. A form of *neged* is used in Genesis 2:18 when Eve is called Adam's *ezer kenegdo*.

Ra (Hebrew, noun or adjective): *wicked, evil, broken.* The first usage of *ra* in the Bible is in the story of Sodom and Gomorrah. The men of the city are pounding at Lot's door, trying to force their way into his house, so they could have sex with the two angels whom he was hosting. "No, my friends," Lot pleads. "Don't do this wicked [*ra*] thing" (Genesis 19:7, NIV). Don't force your way in and break into pieces that which is currently whole. Rape is an accurate and horrifying picture of *ra*. It seeks to destroy and break whole things into pieces.

Racham (Hebrew, verb or noun): When it's a verb, *racham* means "to show deep affection, compassion, or mercy; to protect from harm." This is the fundamental action of God toward God's people, over and over and over again. Deuteronomy 30:3 says, "GOD, your God, will restore everything you lost; he'll have [*racham*] on you; he'll come back and pick up the pieces from all the places where you were scattered" (MSG). When we have a picture of a God who endlessly *racham*s on people, we open ourselves up to the possibility that we can change and that things can change. When it's a noun, it means "womb." What? So to show compassion on someone is like providing a safe place in which he or she can grow and be nourished? God wombs us so we can grow. We womb others so they can grow. See why I love the Hebrew language?

Sehnsucht (German, noun): *the inconsolable longing for something that you are ardently missing but can't quite name.* This is the ache you feel when you see something that needs to change.

Shalom (Hebrew, noun): *peace, wholeness, completeness; a state of being unbroken.* Remember, in the Hebrew, a noun describes a person, place, or thing *in action*. Shalom is much bigger than a state of peace. It describes the movement of God in the world—God is always at work *shaloming*, always making things whole.

Shamar (Hebrew, verb): *to keep, guard, watch, preserve.* Adam and Eve were placed in the Garden of Eden so that they might *shamar* it. They were given this meaningful work from God, and when they were expelled from the Garden, human beings would learn what it meant to *shamar* lots and lots of things, some of which bring life and some of which bring death. What will you keep/guard/watch/preserve with your one and only life? Will it be your own reputation, bank account, waistline, or career? None of those are bad things; they're just not enough to satisfy our deepest longings to guard something more precious. In Numbers 6, the Lord gives instructions for Aaron and the priests to bless the children of Israel by saying that the Lord will *shamar* them. What does it mean to live knowing that you are guarded/kept/watched/preserved by God?

ACKNOWLEDGMENTS

To Mary. Your fierce, restorative love for me guards me and keeps me. Thank you especially for loving me through the gritty and dark season that I was sometimes in while writing this book. And your superb editing made this book so much better.

To my publisher, Don Pape. Thank you for being one of the best human beings I know. Every time I think you've reached the limit of generosity and joy that any one person can possess, you outdo yourself. To my editor, Dave Zimmerman, whose writing prowess is legendary and who finds those elusive gems that remain hidden when I'm writing by myself. To my copyeditor, Helen Macdonald, whose careful eye and gentle suggestions were such a gift at the end of a very long process. To my agent, Chris Ferebee, whose friendship I have come to treasure, whose advice I soak up eagerly, and whose salsa I'm still waiting to taste. To the rest of the NavPress team, thank you for supporting authors like me who insist on using way too much Hebrew. To David

Geeslin, Robin Bermel, and the rest of the team at Tyndale, thank you for your endless creativity in getting this book into people's hands. Your cheerleading and tireless work to get this idea out there gives me a great sense of encouragement.

To my boys—Isaac, Elijah, and Benjamin—for always asking about how my writing is going and for allowing Daddy extra time downstairs to write. Thank you even more for reminding me when it's time to stop and play. I love you to the moon and back, even up to the Death Star and back, even up to God's heart and back. Thanks also for not remaining insistent that I call this book *Middles*.

To Mom and Dad, for listening to me preach, reading my books, and never making me feel anything but supported and loved.

To Jim and Pat, my steadfast in-laws, for your constant prayers and for the way in which you care for your family with such fierce love (and for putting up with your sometimes-too-progressive son-in-law).

To Dave, Julie, Evan, Brody, and Ella. Your family brings me such great joy. I love being with you, laughing with you, answering your deep questions, and kidding with you about stealing your dog. I'm really kidding. Kind of.

To Jeff, Lisa, and Carly. Your little family is bringing so much shalom to the world, and I feel so grateful to be the recipient of some of it. Your thoughtfulness, cheerleading, and compassion help me keep going.

To Joel, Kathy, Halle, and Maggie. The farm! Can you believe that it happened? I believe with all my heart that it will see to the shalom of many people, including me. Every time I'm there, your sweet hospitality gets under my skin (in a good way, of course).

To Adam, Susie, Olivia, and Sophia. You guys. You have been through a lot in the last two years. And through it all, you find a way to love, support, and encourage me and my family in ways that would seem impossible if the shoes were on the other feet. I love you so much.

To Rick and Becky, and Micah and Laura. You know who you are. Thank you for inviting us to gather around your tables so often, and always with such abundance. We feel so lucky to be able to build our nests under your gentle care.

To my dear friends Kyle Jackson, Brad Jackson, Andy Priadka, Stephan Dunning, Stefan Van Voorst, Steve Haines, Steve Person, Charlie Dean, and Matt Ness, who love me as a person and not as a pastor or writer. I'm so grateful for each of you.

To Matt Bays, Erin Lane, Nate Pyle, Dave Hickman, Kevin Butcher, Stu G, and Seth Haines—my writer buddies with whom I share my insecurities. You help me remember why I write, and you help me keep writing.

To Christine Osgood, for providing my monthly home away from home at the Urban Retreat where I can rest, write, breathe, and remember that I'm God's before I'm anything else.

To the courageous congregation and staff at Genesis Covenant Church. Life inside of your loving embrace makes everything better.

And lastly, to my friends Alan and Noah Ullman. These books wouldn't exist without the generative environments you create in which we listen, question, and embody the living Word together. I love you both so much.

NOTES

PREFACE

1. I love this phrase and am indebted to Abarim Publications for it. "Salem meaning," Abarim Publications, accessed February 17, 2017, http://www.abarim-publications.com/Meaning/Salem.html#.VvJ_yhIrKfV.
2. Krista Tippett, *Becoming Wise: An Inquiry into the Mystery and Art of Living* (New York: Penguin, 2016), 29–30.

CHAPTER 1: WHERE ARE YOU?

1. The Enneagram is a centuries-old tool—kind of like a personality test but much more than that—which helps you learn your strengths and shadows. There are nine basic types, all of which respond to the world differently. Read more about the Enneagram in *The Enneagram: A Christian Perspective,* by Richard Rohr and Andreas Ebert (New York: Crossroad, 2001).
2. Seth Haines, *Coming Clean: A Story of Faith* (Grand Rapids, MI: Zondervan, 2015), 14.
3. If you're cynical toward the idea of sin, or if the whole idea of it just feels like a jackhammer to you, please read Francis Spufford's book *Unapologetic: Why, Despite Everything, Christianity Can Still Make Surprising Emotional Sense* (New York: HarperCollins, 2013). I particularly love his definition of sin. He calls it the HPtFtU. You'll have to read the book to see what the acronym means.
4. Richard Rohr, *Yes, and . . . : Daily Meditations* (Cincinnati, OH: Franciscan Media, 2013), 102.

CHAPTER 3: WHAT ARE YOU SEEKING?

1. To hear Kara's sermon, go to "New Beginnings 2016," by Steve Wiens, Jerry Stinar, Kara Groff, Carol Johnsen, and Dan Wanous, January 3, 2016, http://www.genesiscov.org/sundays/sermons/media-item/108/new -beginnings-2016, (8:09).

2. Matt Bays, *Finding God in the Ruins: How God Redeems Pain* (Colorado Springs: David C Cook, 2016).

CHAPTER 4: WHERE ARE YOU GOING?

1. Bruce Feiler, *Abraham: A Journey to the Heart of Three Faiths* (New York: William Morrow, 2005), 22.

2. Ibid., 24–25.

3. For a little more on *lech lecha*, read Rabbi Jeff's illuminating blog post: "Lech Lecha: 'Get Yourself Going,'" October 9, 2013, http://www.rebjeff .com/blog/lech-lecha-get-yourself-going.

4. Thank you for this advice, Eugene Peterson. I had the chance to spend a couple of days with Eugene and Jan in June 2016, and I can tell you that they are spiritual giants on whose shoulders we will sit for many generations to come.

CHAPTER 5: WHAT WILL YOU BRING?

1. Incidentally, "Dubious Claims" would be a killer band name.

2. If you haven't experienced Pete Holmes, you're missing something essential about laughter and joy and being a better human being. Fair warning: If you're offended by foul language, you probably won't enjoy Pete as much as I do.

CHAPTER 6: THE EXODUS

1. Thomas Merton, *Thoughts in Solitude* (New York: Farrar, Straus and Giroux, 1999), 79.

CHAPTER 7: THE WILDERNESS

1. Richard Rohr, *Yes, and . . . : Daily Meditations* (Cincinnati, OH: Franciscan Media, 2013), 114.

2. For research on the idea of the *archegos*, I'm indebted to a great sermon: Martin G. Collins, "Diligence in the Face of Trials," BibleTools.org, January 14, 2006, http://www.bibletools.org/index.cfm/fuseaction/Library .sr/CT/TRANSCRIPT/k/1660.

3. I'm indebted to Henri Nouwen's fantastic book *In the Name of Jesus: Reflections on Christian Leadership* (New York: Crossroad, 1993), 57–60, for this interpretation of the third temptation of Jesus.

NOTES

CHAPTER 8 THE PROMISED LAND

1. Paraphrase of Joshua 1:2-9. This is one of the most stirring examples of God's faithfulness—not just to a person like Joshua but to God's people across the generations.
2. Aren't you glad that *ezer kenegdo*, which means "face-to-face companion who brings strong, powerful, lifesaving help, without which we might die," is the way the Bible describes women when they first break onto the scene?
3. You can find out more about Des Metzler's work at http://www.ceramic restoration.co.za.

EPILOGUE

1. I never thought I'd say I love a denomination, but I love ours: The Evangelical Covenant Church, http://www.covchurch.org.
2. I'm not sure where this invitation originated, but it's readily available online. To access the version we use at Genesis, go to http://www.ststephensrva.org /download_file/view/321/.